Harley-Davidson

THE ALL-AMERICAN MOTORCYCLE

Randy Leffingwell

ISBN-13: 978-0-7603-2733-3
ISBN-10: 0-7603-2733-5

Printed in China

On the cover: Where the other Softail models reprised the look of Harley's past, the Deuce, Harley's latest addition to its Softail line, forged a super-custom look for Harley's future. The Deuce is powered by a counterbalanced version of the Motor Company's most modern air-cooled engine, the Twin Cam 88B™.

On the frontispiece: Faded glory. The Model J introduced a three-speed transmission, electric lighting, and a mechanical oil pump to the Harley line. The version shown is from 1917.

On the title page: The 1971 FX Super Glide was one of Willie G.'s earlier, more dramatic styling exercises. Known as the "Night Train," its boat-tail rear fender/seat section was its most recognizable feature.

On the back cover: The predecessor to the 1956 KHKs was the Model K, introduced in 1952 to replace the long-lived, and by then, long-in-the-tooth, Model WL.

Contents

Dedication

For the late Otis Chandler and the late Jerry Sewell.

Foreword

From the title of this book, I hope you will understand what it is and more importantly what it is not. I have left to experts such as Jerry Hatfield and Harry V. Sucher the telling of technical and engineering histories of Harley-Davidson motorcycles. I have left to fine writers and careful researchers Allan Girdler and Stephen Wright the histories of racing and riding. I have left to insightful historian David Wright the saga of the company.

I am enormously indebted to these historians for their experience and scholarship. This book, however, is not meant to be any of theirs. Yet it has required me to make small and occasional skirmish raids into their domains in order to place in context what it is that I have taken on—the emotional appeal of these magnificent machines.

Acknowledgements

First and foremost, my greatest thanks go to the late Otis Chandler and his widow Bettina Chandler, Ojai, California. The first vehicle Otis owned was a Harley-Davidson while he was in college in the 1950s. For a time, the collection he assembled at his Vintage Museum in Oxnard, California, honored the mystique as well as his own tradition. All of the motorcycles in this book, except for those specifically identified otherwise, belong to the Chandlers. Without their extremely enthusiastic cooperation, this book would not have been possible.

I am grateful to Art Gompper, Manager, Racing Promotions, Harley-Davidson Motorcycle Company, for his assistance with access to the new VR1000 factory racing motorcycles, and to Sears Point International Raceway for their generous cooperation.

I am greatly indebted to Daniel Statnekov, Tesuque, New Mexico, for their kindness, inspiration, and cooperation.

I want to thank Mr. Phil Cooper, Vice President, Public Relations and Advertising, Caesars Palace, Las Vegas, Nevada, and Debbie Munch, Director of Public Relations, for their help and cooperation. And I am very grateful to Gary Graham, Las Vegas, for access to Evel Knievel's Wembley Stadium Jump motorcycle.

I also want to thank Thomas R. Kowalksi, Englewood, Colorado, for his generous access to his collection and especially to his 1912 belt-drive twin.

In addition, thanks to Glendale, Arizona, Harley-Davidson and to Bernie Stewart, Glendale, Arizona, for access to his 1995 Buell S-2 Thunderbolt.

At the risk of confusion, I also thank Oliver A. Shokouh, president of Glendale (California), Harley-Davidson, for access to his 1977 Low Rider.

I am grateful to Edwin Deegan, Philadelphia, Pennsylvania, for his recollections of the 358th Bomber Squadron at Molesworth, England. And to Claire Olson, Livingston, Montana, for his reminiscences of miles on the road.

In addition, I want to thank Doug Dullenkopf, President, Screaming Eagle Aircraft Sales, Santa Paula, California; Dave Hansen, proprietor of The Shop-American Motorcycle Specialists, Ventura, California; Katherine Hulme, President, Santa Maria Museum of Flight, Santa Maria, California; Bill and Stephanie Huth, Willow Springs International Raceway, Rosamond, California; William Lenox, Oxnard, California; Andy Mendez, Top Dead Center, Oxnard, California; Jim Naylor, Ventura Raceway, Ventura, California; John and Kenny Newton, Modesto, California; and Dean Walsh, Oxnard, California.

I must thank Zack Miller, my editor at the time and now MBI Publisher, technical editor, Greg Field, and my friend Michael Dregni, for the opportunity to do this book.

I thank David Wright for his long friendship, his clear vision, and his sparkling perspectives.

Last of all—but most of all—I am deeply indebted to the late Jerry Sewell, General Manager of the Vintage Museum, and my kind and generous friend. Jerry restored several of the Harley-Davidson motorcycles in the Vintage Museum collection. More importantly, his involvement with Harley-Davidson is life-long. His perspectives and ideas helped me immeasurably in understanding and attempting to portray the Myth and Mystique of Harley-Davidson.

May you all ride many safe miles.

—*Randy Leffingwell*
Santa Barbara, California

Introduction

A myth is a story told and retold. The best storytellers enhance and embellish the tale a little bit with each recounting. They personalize it, embellishing or tailoring some portions of it in order to evoke a quicker, stronger response from their listeners.

Eventually, many of the great myth stories are written down. This happens not so much to finalize the story as to make it available to a wider audience. But most of the myths—of the Greek gods, of the Chinese fire-breathing dragons, of the two boys raised by wolves who grew up to found the city of Rome—were told and improved upon for centuries before they were codified. Modern-day readers can scarcely imagine what the original event may have been, how different it was from what now appears printed on paper and bound in cloth.

It is only because of mass communications that myths can be etched in stone overnight and circulated worldwide the next morning. Historical fabrications and creative inventions and wild stories can pass from the state of fiction into fact and then on into legend within hours. Even in the late 1940s, all it took to launch a legend was a couple of journalists arriving in a small town several hours after an event had concluded. What could they do if they were assigned by their editor to get a story that had ended before they ever left their office?

And so it was, in the late editions of the July 5, 1947, *San Francisco Chronicle*, that the mystique of motorcycling in the United States became codified as the myth of July Fourth in Hollister. The tale had young fearless beasts carrying off fair maidens. It had roaring, fire-breathing machines terrorizing the helpless citizenry of a small village. And, just as is the case with nearly all myths, it actually had an element or two of truth in its printed version.

But because of telephone lines and mass media, this myth achieved phenomenal impact almost overnight. All motorcyclists became something to be feared. Hollister's own newspaper played a part in establishing the "biker" myth of motorcycling.

But its impact was negligible compared to what happened when an alert picture editor at *Life* magazine noticed a nighttime flash shot inching its way out of the wire photo machine. A blubbery, boozy, squint-eyed guy straddled a Harley-Davidson. He and the bike were parked, so the caption stated, in front of Johnnies Tavern in Hollister, California. The man in the photo hoisted a beer bottle in each hand. The street and curb beneath him were littered with empties. The caption identified him, generically, as one of several thousand who had invaded the town on the holiday weekend. For the *Life* picture editor, it was just the kind of image that begged for cover treatment. This was the kind of photo that would cry out to passersby: "Pick up this magazine. Buy it! Read it and grow fearful." (Widespread home-delivered subscriptions were still a thing of the future; newsstand sales constituted the majority of all publications' access to readers.)

So *Life* magazine, on deadline on a Sunday night, with no time to call California to check the facts, ran the myth of Hollister on its cover. The motto for most mythmakers—and some journalists in times past—probably has been, "Never let the facts get in the way of a good story." *Life* shipped out millions of copies to trusting, unsuspecting readers.

Within a week, anyone on a motorcycle was the overweight beer drinker on the cover of *Life*. Any rider was one of the rioters of Hollister.

It took 20 years to soften the myth. It required Honda to adopt a marketing program that advertised that "you meet the nicest people" on a motorcycle before the damaging effects of that fabricated photo and its exaggerated story began to erode. A few years after that campaign, Harley-Davidson recognized that nice people can ride any motorcycle they want. Its own product line became diluted and homogenized to meet the marketplace of the Age of Aquarius.

But it was the people who already lived the great myth—or wanted to make new ones of their own—who were keeping the company and its product alive. It was these loyalists that Willie

G. Davidson, grandson of one of the founders, recognized. It was to these people and in their honor that he began to direct his creative efforts.

The results are a story everyone knows. That Harley-Davidson saved itself from extinction by its own devices and through the last minute help of a few close friends is now a part of the mythology of modern business. That Willie G. Davidson's designs evoke the era when "all" serious, dedicated bikers had a police record in Hollister—or Oakland, or San Bernardino—has steadily and reliably paid dividends to Davidson, the company, its dealers and shareholders, and to its riders alike. It is the myth of Hollister—and other legendary renegade and rebellious incidents—that Harley-Davidson caters to now.

Historian and writer David Wright, a perceptive man with a dry, quick wit who is as familiar with the mystique as anyone, has mused that Harley's typical recent customer is "an actuarial aching to be bad." For 30 years, Wright observed, actual bad guys supported the company by buying its products. Those hard-times customers with two- and three-syllable nicknames now have been largely supplanted by Walter Mittys with two- and three-letter titles after their name—MD, CEO, or PhD.

On any given Sunday at The Rock Store in Malibu, California, generally between noon and 4:00 p.m., the crowd of Harley riders mingles with the group of Harley wannabees. A newcomer asks a veteran about one model after another, wondering about size, power, and cost. He finally confides the he always had wanted one and now, as a successful, and overworked professional, his therapist and his wife have told him that he "needs" to get a Harley and go for a ride. At The Rock Store and at hundreds of other weekend half-day travel destinations, riders and soon-to-be owners who wear wing-tip Florsheim shoes, three-piece Brooks Brothers suits, and club ties on weekdays wriggle into black leather, tie a black-and-orange bandanna around their head, and become somebody else.

In one corner of the parking lot in Malibu, a heavyset rider pounded up and down on the kickstarter. A crowd gathers. They were impressed by the age of the bike and the dedication of the rider. The bike coughed without conviction. The group grew, drawn by curiosity. The kicker was one of those who kept Harley-Davidson alive during the bleak years. A dozen yards away, another rider turned a key, flipped a switch, and twisted his wrist a few times. The engine ripped to life. The key-turner dropped a toe, gently released the clutch, and eased his way out onto "the black ribbon," Mulholland Highway, the sinuous road that runs past The Rock Store. Behind him the kicker continued. His huge frame rose and fell in a kind of intercourse against the kickstarter's resistance. Out on the highway, turning gently west, the key-turner spun his right hand. The twin pipes bellowed, turning heads. That noise always draws attention. And still the kicker kicked.

As if to answer the question everyone has feared to ask a man who truly looks bad, he tried another kick and called out to no one in particular:

"It's got a mag, maaaaan ...."

Another kick and the magneto—its spark-making contribution finally acknowledged—made electricity. The engine erupted, rending the air with the same staccato two-cylinder thunder. But it somehow was much louder, more fearsome because of the amazing labor it took to call it forth. Leaves on the ground behind his twin fishtail exhaust pipes blasted angrily against the rock walls and whirled furiously into the air. The kicker, sweat on his face and arms, settled himself heavily on to this long-unyielding bike. He worked the throttle with the dexterity of a pinball wizard. He—just like the key-turner long moments before him—threaded his way through the crowd of other riders and other Harley-Davidsons. And when he reaches the road, he turned and—without glancing back at the crowd still watching him and headed resolutely east—he dropped the bike into gear, released the clutch, and nailed the throttle. With a noise that Thor, the mythological Norse God of Thunder, proudly would call his own, the kicker shattered the air in Malibu.

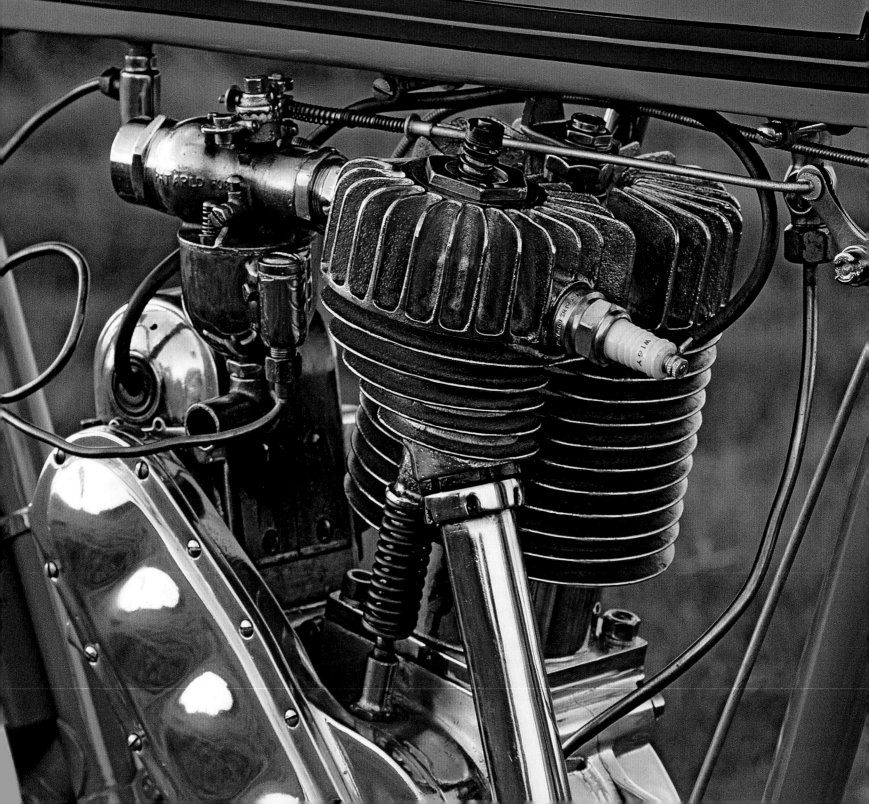

Chapter 1
The First Decade 1903–1912

They were like most modern-day entrepreneurs. Bill Harley and Arthur Davidson saw a need and seized the opportunity. The need was for basic transportation. And the opportunity came in the form of a bicycle frame and a French-designed DeDion-Bouton single-cylinder gasoline engine.

It was 1900. America hadn't met the automobile, let alone fallen in love. Henry Ford had not yet opened his doors, and his heart belonged more to farm tractors than to automobiles. Most of the world still got about by horses and bicycles or, over longer distances, by steam locomotives or ships. The Wright brothers had not yet proven flight was possible, against the wind, on a North Carolina beach. But gasoline-powered internal combustion was ready. It was the eve of revolutionizing the Industrial Revolution.

In 1900, William S. Harley was a 20-year-old apprentice draftsman. His lifelong friend, Arthur Davidson, was 19 and already working as a pattern maker. Both were employed at Barth Manufacturing, a metal fabricating company in Milwaukee. Like most working men in the world, they commuted to work on bicycles, and they followed the widely popular professional bicycle racing events. But as companies in the eastern states began clipping engines onto pedal bicycles, the two friends—both technically oriented—got caught up in the idea of the motorcycle. And by 1901, they began to try to make their own.

Theirs was like any cottage industry that moonlights after the day-job is done. Progress was slow. Two years passed. They had not completed a single machine while companies such as Indian, Pope, Thor, and others had machines in production. In late April 1903, older brother Walter came home for Arthur's wedding. Walter worked in Parsons, Kansas, for one

Above: Harley-Davidson took special pride in its new optional color. Up until 1906, Arthur Davidson and Bill Harley's motorcycles were available only in piano black. But that year, the company introduced Renault Gray, appropriated from the French car company, and set it off with carmine striping.

Opposite: The first Harley-Davidson engines were closely based on the French DeDion-Bouton atmospheric-intake-valve, one-piece cylinder design. The head was part of the cylinder barrel. The intake valve sat directly over the exhaust in a pocket alongside the cylinder/combustion chamber, a design known as intake over exhaust (IOE), or pocket valve.

This is the Model 8-A, a four-horsepower, single-cylinder motorcycle. It sold at the factory in 1912 for $225 and was capable of 45 miles per hour at the hands of a brave and daring rider. The bike was built on a 51-inch wheelbase.

of the railroads, as an apprentice machinist in their tool shop. Frustrated by the kind of work he saw one of his brother's hired men performing, Walter took over.

By late 1903, Henry Ford was in business, the Wright brothers had flown, and there was a feeling in American cities that this was going to be a different century, a great century, a century of progress. No one had any idea yet what that meant, but the visionary and the ambitious across the nation were getting antsy.

Arthur got married and Walter returned to Kansas but not for long. Soon he was back in Milwaukee, working his nights and weekends for his brother after working days for another railroad in their shops. Within a few weeks, the first motorcycle was ready to ride. A modified bicycle frame—given a loop to support the engine where the front crank and pedals would have been—held the small single-cylinder engine. With total displacement of only 10.2 cubic inches, the horsepower was all of three.

Harley and the Davidson brothers included a bicycle crank and pedals on their first machine. This was part of the starting procedure. Riders pedaled the nearly 200-pound motorcycle up to "speed" and then gradually released a tensioning wheel that slackened the leather drive belt connecting the engine to the rear wheel. Engine compression, released by a hand-operated valve, allowed the engine to turn, and as soon as it fired, riders shut off the compression valve, and then took their feet off the pedals and puttered away. But the pedals were there not only to get

the machine underway. Three horsepower was not enough to get the motorcycle and rider up Milwaukee's few hills. Braking also required the pedals because Harley and Davidson used a bicycle-type rear coaster brake. Arthur Davidson, Bill Harley, and Walter Davidson painted it black, named the motorcycle Harley-Davidson, and tested their prototype fairly thoroughly. But over time, they learned that bicycle frames were not strong enough; their adopted frame distorted or broke several times, and its steering-head bearings failed frequently.

The boys had already conceived of improvements for a second version. Their first change was to move from the Davidson family garage to a friend's shop. Next was a new engine, larger, with total displacement of 24.7 cubic inches. The second prototype and then the third motorcycle, their first "production" model—the first one meant to be sold—were begun almost immediately. Late in 1903, the second prototype was complete. It also used a bicycle frame, and its failures pointed out that what was really needed next was a new frame. Arthur Davidson and Bill Harley designed the new chassis from scratch. By the end of 1903, Arthur and Walter Davidson's father, William C., a cabinetmaker, demonstrated his confidence in the boy's efforts and became their first investor. He built for them a 10-by-15-foot wood shed behind their home at 38th Street and Highland Avenue.

In 1904, the three Davidsons (sons and father) and Harley sold their first "Harley-Davidson" motorcycle. The bike was named in that order because it had been Bill Harley's initial idea and he had done most of the prototype testing. History doesn't record that first customer's full name, but a Mr. Meyer must have been well satisfied because he put 6,000 miles on his Harley-Davidson before he sold it. Word spread slowly and orders trickled into the new company. A second production motorcycle was completed in 1904. With regular production looming on the horizon, Bill Harley left the business to attend the University of Wisconsin–Madison to study automotive engineering.

The Harley-Davidson engine was a fairly simple and common affair for the day. Having studied the designs available, the boys cast their own block and heads. They chose the atmospheric-intake-valve design. Set at the top of the pocket, the valve was sucked straight down on the intake stroke. As the piston came back up, the pressure shoved the valve shut. The exhaust valve was set into the side of the cylinder and operated by camshaft and connecting rods at the appropriate time. This was known as intake-over-exhaust (IOE) and is frequently described as an F-head design (the intake manifold and exhaust pipe forming somewhat parallel horizontal lines off the vertical cylinder). There were more advanced ideas and designs under scrutiny around the world, but the Harley-Davidson men lacked the spare cash needed to experiment. The F-head IOE system was common, simple, and reliable.

More interest in the Harley-Davidson motorcycle prompted the next developments in early 1905. The backyard "factory" doubled in size. Walter Davidson left his day job to become the company's first full-time manager (and its only full-time employee). Brother Arthur became Harley-Davidson's sales manager. Then Walter hired a part-time worker, and eight motorcycles were completed and sold.

Harley-Davidsons were already competing for recognition and titles, too. On July 4, 1905, in Chicago, one of their bikes covered 15 miles in 19 minutes and 2 seconds.

In 1906, business multiplied, and 50 motorcycles were sold. Arthur sent letters to prospective customers, and in that same year, catalogs displayed the motorcycle in great detail. In 1907, after 150 bikes were sold, the Motorcycle Company was joined by Arthur's oldest brother, William A. (who also left a railroad tool shop job), and the company incorporated as The Harley-Davidson Motor Company.

The company grew sharp as it grew large. An uncle loaned them money to buy land in an industrial district of Milwaukee, and they built a 28-by-80-foot shop at 37th and Chestnut. (The factory never moved again. Years later, Chestnut was renamed Juneau Avenue.) Harley-Davidson's production motorcycles were fitted with exhaust mufflers from the start, and when the company offered a gray paint scheme to the product lineup for 1906, Arthur advertised the machine as the "Silent Gray Fellow."

In 1907, competition became a greater consideration. There were many firms in business making motorcycles, most all of

A Bosch ZE1 magneto fired the 35 ci, single-cylinder engine. The drive pulley was available in 4.50-, 5.25-, and 6.00-inch diameters, all leather-lined. The large lever tightened an idler wheel against the drive pulley, acting as a kind of clutch.

them similar to the Harley-Davidson machines. Some, however, were slapped together by barely competent bicycle repairmen and very talented get-rich-quick schemers. These machines frequently broke within their first dozen miles, shaken to pieces. Or their front forks shattered after the first few impacts with the potholes that dotted American roads. Harleys held up better thanks to their leading-link front fork—a design that would remain a company feature for more than 40 years.

The better machines that held together usually entered organized competitions to demonstrate their abilities. In mid-September, Walter Davidson entered a two-day, 414-mile endurance run from Chicago, Illinois, to Kokomo, Indiana. Twenty-three riders started, and Walter was one of three who finished with perfect point scores. By year's end, this reliability and performance had led more than 150 committed buyers to the company's doors.

Before the end of 1907, Bill Harley had accomplished his most notable—but least known—experiment. He had built his first two-cylinder engine. Historian David Wright, researching for his book *The Harley-Davidson Motor Company*, uncovered references to the engine. But even as a Harley engineering experiment, it must have been disappointing. Beyond the brief reference, Wright found no details about the effort.

In 1908, the company tripled sales to around 450 motorcycles, and the factory doubled again and then again in size—up now to nearly 4,800 square feet. Employees also doubled and redoubled, first to 18 and then to 36. In 1909, when

Above: The wire pull that runs up past the toolbox operated an exhaust cutout. This would allow a slight horsepower increase and a definite noise increase. Otherwise Harley and Davidson prided themselves on the effective mufflers of their early motorcycles. It is ironic to think of today's thunderous Big-Twins as the latest evolution of a company that boastfully produced the "Silent Gray Fellow" 80 years ago.

Opposite: The 1.75-inch-wide leather belt drove the 20-inch-diameter rear pulley. Standard tires were 2.25x28 inches. A bicycle-type coaster rear brake, operated by staggered pedals attempted to cease forward movement.

Right: This is the Silent Gray Fellow's twin-cylinder brother, the Model X-8-D. It sold new in 1912 for $285. Wheelbase was increased to 56.50 inches, 5.50 inches longer than the single-cylinder motorcycles.

Right: The two-cylinder engine measured 49.5 cubic inches from a bore and stroke of 3.0x3.5 inches. Harley claimed 6.5 horsepower. The cylinder and cylinder heads—still cast as one piece—used mechanical intake valves.

Opposite: The twins used a Bosch magneto and a Schebler carburetor. The crankcase was aluminum while the cylinders and heads were nickel-plated cast iron (to prevent rusting).

Bill Harley came home from school in Madison for a visit, he stayed long enough to put on paper the plans for the company's first successful production twin, essentially their existing single with a second cylinder grafted onto the rear.

Arthur Davidson took to the road, wearing his marketer's hat. He interviewed and examined potential dealers. Through the course of the next year, he learned that both the government and private enterprise had discovered uses for motorcycles. Up to that point, though, only his competitors had secured contracts. Arthur took a demonstration machine to the Rural Free Delivery Mail Carriers national convention. There he began what would become a very long-lasting relationship between U.S. government agencies and Harley-Davidson.

William Harley graduated from the university with honors and returned to the factory. He began immediately to make improvements to the Silent Gray Fellow. He strengthened the frame and lengthened the wheelbase from 51 inches to 57 inches and increased displacement of the new single-cylinder atmospheric-valve engine to early 35 cubic inches. With five horsepower available at the twist of a wrist, the Harley-Davidson motorcycle could reach 50 miles per hour. They tested it as a prototype in 1909 and called it the Model 5-35; some say it was named for its horsepower and displacement while others content the "5" referred to Harley-Davidson's fifth year of sales.

The reliability and strength that the Davidsons developed, tested, and built into their machines was beginning to pay off. Sales nearly tripled to 1,149 in 1909 and doubled to 3,168 in 1910, then rose to 5,625 in 1911 and then rose again to 9,571 in 1912. The first buyer, Mr. Meyer had sold his motorcycle. By 1912 it had gone through another five owners, and it had accumulated more than 62,000 miles. In an era when companies rose, flourished, failed, and disappeared within months, whether manufacturing automobiles, motorcycles, farm tractors, or even airplanes, Harley-Davidson was steadily—if rapidly—building a reputation.

It was competition—in the marketplace and on the dirt roads and tracks—that established Harley-Davidson's name. Walter Davidson willingly assisted Arthur Davidson's marketing efforts by virtue of his dozens of victories in a variety of endurance events and even some all-out races.

In 1908, Walter did well enough in a national endurance race that he scored not only a perfect 1,000 points, but he earned an additional 5 for consistency. Real racing began by 1910. Daredevils appeared on banked indoor bicycle race ovals that were made of wood planks. At first these were tiny tracks of an eighth or a sixth of a mile. But they quickly grew into specially made motorcycle board tracks of a quarter and a third of a mile. And speed challenges were now common additions to county and state fairs, kicking up and scattering the dirt on half- and one-mile horse tracks. Victories against Pope, Indian, and Excelsior had begun to clear out the also-rans, the Johnny-come-lately's, and the fly-by-night schemers. In Harley-Davidson's first 10 years in operation, more than 75 firms went into the motorcycle business and out.

Between 1909 and 1912, Arthur Davidson continued to promote sales and William Harley worked on development and testing. The models they offered in 1912 were the first noticeable

Above: The drive belt for the twins was made of two-ply leather, 1.75 inches wide. The brakes were still simply bicycle-type rear coaster brakes operated by back pedaling. The Universal Tire Company tires—2.5x26 inches—were white because tire makers had not yet begun to use carbon black in their chemical blends.

Opposite: Harley-Davidson designated this the Model X-8-D to denote that it had not only an idler to adjust the belt but a clutch as well. The twin without the clutch was simply the 8-D and sold for $10 less. The X-8-E offered a chain drive in addition to the clutch and also sold for $285.

step away from the bicycle appearance. They took the top rail, horizontal on a bicycle, and inclined it down toward the rear wheel. This lowered the riding height, and it enabled the seat post to accommodate a spring to absorb rear-wheel shocks.

One of Bill Harley's interests during the preceding years was the clear mechanical advantages of chain drive. But without any way to gently engage the power, even five horsepower was too hard on running gear. After several years of experimentation, he settled on using a multiplate clutch. He linked it to a control lever on the left side of the left tank. This operated a rod-and bell-crank mechanism. A free-wheeling-type clutch housed within the rear hub was thoroughly tested and then offered—mated to a chain drive—on late-production bikes in the 1912 model year.

For riders, the improvement was significant. Previously, starting the motorcycle meant pedaling furiously and slowly tightening the tension wheel against the leather belt. Although a rider still put the motorcycle up on its rear stand and pedaled furiously, the clutch now remained engaged. The engine started without the load of its rider plus the motorcycle's weight. Once the engine was warmed up, the clutch was disengaged, the rider rocked the machine forward off the stand, re-engaged the clutch, and rode away. Belt slippage in wet weather was no longer a problem. And a drive system was in place that could effectively handle the additional power of the Harley-designed twins.

That 1907 two-cylinder engine couldn't have been a total failure. The twin surfaced again in 1909. It simply had teething problems that Harley-Davidson believed it had fixed when regular series production of two-cylinder motorcycles began in 1911. (Those problems related to valves and were serious enough to keep twins off the market in 1910.) The 1909 and 1911 engines were basically the single-cylinder models with a second-cylinder grafted on at a 45-degree angle. Where the 1909 model used section-type intake valves, the 1911 used mechanical intake valves opened by tappets that were driven off a pinion in the engine case. Earliest production twins displaced just about 49.5 cubic inches. Then, while the 3.50-inch stroke remained unchanged, buyers had an option beginning with the 1912 models of either 3.00-inch bore or 3.31-inch bore that increased total engine capacity to the legendary 60.32 cubic inches.

Carburetion had been a challenge to Harley-Davidson even before its first production bikes were built. It was solved initially by working with Ole Evinrude (the other significant Milwaukee engine-builder). Harley-Davidson soon developed its own carburetor that worked well enough on its motorcycles until Schebler Carburetor Company began to produce models specifically for motorcycles. (Schebler was more widely known for producing carburetors for farm tractors; however, its Model H was offered as an optional carburetor for H-D's short-lived 1909 twin prototypes.) Harley-Davidson claimed a 65-mile-per-hour top speed was possible from its 60 ci, seven-horsepower

engine. The frame was significantly strengthened to handle the additional power.

In order to make a two-cylinder engine, only two configurations were possible. There was not much space available to motorcycle builders. A side-by-side twin would be too wide and bulky. The vee-configuration was the necessary choice. According to Harry Sucher, author of *Harley Davidson; The Milwaukee Marvel*, engine power would nearly double while adding much less than double the weight—something like an additional 30 to 35 pounds. But because the two cylinders had to fit within the triangular confines of these modified bicycle frames, the narrow angle of 45 degrees was required. The tight confines also limited the cylinder bore. To increase power, engines had to grow in displacement; to increase displacement, the piston's stroke had to increase. This limited the speed at which the engine could operate because at high rpm the piston accelerations were so high at each end of its stroke that the forces created could overstress pistons, connecting rods, and the crankpins. But long-stroke engines had one sterling attribute that compensated for the rpm limitations: they developed great amounts of torque at lower speeds.

So Bill Harley worked within the limitations of long strokes and took advantage of the low-speed torque to design a slow-revving engine that would run a long time between major overhauls. He engineered the nearly simultaneous arrival of both pistons to the top of the cylinders. (If the motorcycle was viewed from the right, the flywheels would spin clockwise. Harley's design brought the rear piston to the top 45 degrees of flywheel rotation ahead of the front piston.) This endowed the engines with two lasting effects: the vibration and the exhaust sound for which Harley-Davidson became famous.

The foundations of the legend were in place.

While it still resembled a bicycle frame, it was beginning to be more of a motorcycle frame. The loop running beneath the engine ran continuously down from the steering head and back up to the seat tube. The seat, suspended at the front, was supported by a spring shaft. It was known as the "Ful-Floteing" seat and was introduced in 1912.

Chapter 2
Improvements

In 1913, as a result of dealer pressure, customer wishes, and public interest in racing, Harley-Davidson's engineering department threw its hat into the ring. Chief Engineer William Harley hired Bill Ottaway to be his assistant. At the time, Ottaway was the chief engineer of Thor Motorcycle Division of Aurora Automatic Machine Company of Aurora, Illinois. Ottaway's "White Thors" had competed against Harley-Davidson not only on the roads but against Harley-Davidson's customers on their own privately entered souped-up motorcycles. Ottaway's first task was to concentrate on speed tuning which allowed William Harley to turn his attention to the transmission. (William had finished last in a prestigious desert endurance race from San Diego to Phoenix in 1909 largely because his racer had but one speed.)

Although Ottaway was hired to engineer (and manage) the racing operations, Harley knew that other racing developments would benefit the road bikes. Multiple-speed transmissions weren't just a racing necessity. Harley-Davidson had introduced an optional sidecar—for an additional $75—that allowed the cyclist to carry a friend as well as some baggage. The extra load required multiple gears to make best use of the engine's power and torque. The engineering commitment to the sidecar was not unwarranted. Ford's Model T, introduced in 1909, was still selling for $850 in 1912. So Harley-Davidson's advantage—roughly half the price—was significant.

Harley-Davidson sales in 1909 had numbered more than 1,100 motorcycles, produced by some 100 employees in a four-acre factory site. Motorcycling was immensely popular. The marketplace, winnowed down to about 36 makes, by and large produced reliable machines of consistent quality. At the end of 1913, Harley-Davidson recorded nearly 71,000 sales.

Above: The golden age of the sidecar was upon America, and Harley manufactured its own at this time. Standard sidecar practice cocked the motorcycle slightly towards the sidecar. This was disconcerting to a first-time rider, but it aided steering and handling greatly. A total of 9,180 Model Js were sold in 1917 for $310. For an additional $80, the Model 17-L "standard pleasure sidecar" could be included.

Opposite: The 1940 Boeing Stearman A75-N1 (PT-17) followed the Harley Model 17-J by a generation. Around Santa Paula, California, Screamin' Eagle aircraft sales' two-place Stearman flies circles around most things in the air. Of course, the Stearman uses a nine-cylinder radial overhead-valve Pratt & Whitney Wasp Junior engine that puts out 450 horsepower. That's some 28 times the power of a two-place Harley Model 17-J.

Above: The three-speed transmission was shifted by the left hand while the left foot operated a pedal-type clutch similar to the clutch used in automobiles. The optional speedometer, missing its glass, was driven by a bull-and-pinion gear on the rear-wheel hub.

Opposite: In 1915, Harley-Davidson introduced the Model J twin with a bore and stroke of 3.43x3.50 inches, for a total displacement of 60.33 cubic inches. Improvements introduced on the Model J included a three-speed transmission, electric lighting, and a mechanical oil pump. Harley-Davidson rated the new twin at 11 horsepower. In 1917, the Model J was fitted with the four-lobe cam from the eight-valve racer, and Harley advertised the Model J engines as having 16 horsepower. This 1917 Model J, was officially designated the Model 17-J by the manufacturer.

For the 1915 street motorcycles, H-D introduced the step starter to replace the bicycle chain and gear. William Harley's work on transmissions had resulted in a two-speed gear fitted into the rear hub. It was shifted by a lever along the left side of the tank, and it was available as an option on the Silent Gray Fellows. In addition, he introduced a three-speed version for the twin-cylinder bikes; however this transmission was fitted behind the engine. All the two-cylinder motorcycles had benefited from Bill Ottaway's racing knowledge and experience. Power output for street twins had increased by more than a third.

In racing and on the roads, Harley-Davidson watched the competition fade into the distance. While more than 200,000 motorcycles had been registered since the turn of the century, motorcycle manufacturing by 1916 had narrowed to the Big Three. Indian, founded before Harley, was still the leader and continuing to grow. Excelsior Motorcycles had been founded and funded by Ignatz Schwinn who continued to make his fortune in human-powered cycles. Schwinn's backing ensured Excelsior's health. Harley-Davidson was considered solid because of Arthur Davidson's marketing skills and William Davidson's production control. Davidson obsessively promoted production efficiency and quality control.

In 1916, H-D replaced the step-start with the kick-start mechanism that would fire bikes to life for nearly six more decades. Meanwhile Arthur Davidson's early marketing efforts with the U.S. government paid off. The U.S. Army invaded Mexico with 20,000 men, led by General John J. Pershing, to find Mexican renegade General Pancho Villa. Villa, with the advantage of local knowledge of the terrain, was never captured, but Pershing's effort was the first time the Army was motorized—on motorcycles, automobiles, trucks, tractors, and overhead in aircraft. The Army spread its contract over the Big Three, using bikes with and without sidecars. While the goal was not met, The Army—curious about replacing horses for cavalry and artillery units—viewed the entire operation as a success.

During the fall of 1916, Arthur Davidson launched a new marketing effort. A company publication, *The Dealer*, had been sent to its sales force. It was replaced with *The Enthusiast*. This new publication would go to all registered Harley-Davidson owners as well as dealers. In this way, H-D not only informed dealers of new models and developments, it also encouraged its owner to continue as customers.

World War I had interrupted the expansion of the H-D dealer network in Europe. The market seemed interested even though barely 350 motorcycles were sold up until mid-1914. About this time, the war became a great concern in the United States. Racing was suspended.

Author Harry V. Sucher examined the period and found that war preparedness profoundly recast history for the Big Three motorcycle manufacturers. Indian had been run since 1913 by profit-oriented, nonriding directors. It believed that

the wartime military needs would guarantee the company's income whereas civilian markets would tighten. According to Sucher, Indian cut motorcycle prices to $187.50 for cycles and $49.50 for sidecars. It offered the government 20,000 units at those prices. Indian expected its profits would come from the quantity sold. They were willing to eliminate the civilian market and its competition with other makes that required advertising and promotion as well as dealer support.

Harley-Davidson approached it from the opposite view. Accepting the necessity of military participation, it also understood that its position—currently second behind Indian in civilian sales—would improve if Indian produced only government bikes. So Harley-Davidson offered the government 7,000 units—at Indian's price—but it kept production set for another 10,000 bikes for the home market. Arthur Davidson then lavishly promoted Harley's military effort and vigorously pursued new retail dealers, especially in areas previously known to be hostile Indian territory.

It worked.

Indian sold nearly three-times as many motorcycles to the government as Harley-Davidson did, 41,000 versus 15,000. But when

Above: Harley introduced a new color, "military drab," during the 1917 model year. A darker green color was used for the ever-present pinstriping. On early-1917 production models, the crankcase and transmission remained gray but by midyear, it was all olive drab.

Left: Tires were 2.5x28 inches from Goodyear or Firestone. Standard motorcycles were fitted with a 15-tooth engine sprocket while the sidecar engines used 14 teeth to take better advantage of the engine power range. Buyers had to specify the combination, however, when ordering a sidecar.

the war ended, Indian's dealer organization had scattered. Many of them had gone with Harley-Davidson in order to stay in business.

Harley had introduced its Model J in 1915 before America entered the war. It was the next step in advancing the twin-cylinder motorcycles. With the Model J, the two-speed hub transmission was replaced with the three-speed version, using a multiple-plate clutch. The motorcycle's ride was improved because the gears and clutch were now located next to the engine. This moved the weight, still without suspension to carry it, to the center of the bike, improving balance.

Following the war, the Js received numerous improvements, some as a result of prewar racing development and others as part of wartime military and civilian experiences. Among other changes, new intake manifolds, improved cams, stronger valve gears, and a larger oil pump gave the motorcycle nearly a 25 percent power increase. More noticeable was the change of the stamping dies used for the fuel and oil tanks that straddled the top tube. The square edges were rounded. It began another trend that would stay with Harley-Davidson throughout its life as hard edges continued to soften and stretch out.

Chapter 3
A Detour

The second decade of Harley-Davidson's life had brought profound changes to the United States and to the world. In 1913, federal income tax was forced on Americans through the Sixteenth Amendment, and Henry Ford introduced the assembly line. In 1914, the "war to end all wars" began, and the Panama Canal opened. In 1915, Albert Einstein proposed his General Theory of Relativity, film maker D. W. Griffith produced *Birth Of A Nation*, and Henry Ford produced his millionth automobile and sold his first farm tractor. In 1916, daylight-saving time was introduced in England, Frank Lloyd Wright designed the Imperial Hotel in Tokyo, and the National Park Service was established.

In 1917, George M. Cohan wrote *Over There*, and Sigmund Freud published his *Introduction to Psychoanalysis*. In 1918, the U.S. population reached 103.5 million; airmail was established between New York, Washington, and Chicago; and November 30, after nearly 8.5 million deaths, World War I ended. The Eighteenth Amendment to the Constitution in 1919 prohibited the sale of alcoholic beverages, and the Black Sox brought shame to baseball.

In April 1919, Harley-Davidson plunged into this sea of change with the introduction of the Model W Sport Twin. It introduced a completely new horizontal, opposed two-cylinder 30 ci, six-horsepower engine. Its three-speed transmission was incorporated within the cases, with its flywheel mounted outside. The final drive chain was fully enclosed in stamped sheet metal. Harley's normal front suspension with its leading link was changed for the Sport Twin; a single barrel coil spring was attached to the front head to support a trailing link strut fork. The bike weighed barely 275 pounds.

Above: This flat, opposed twin that powered the Model W was fed by a Schebler carburetor. The intake and exhaust manifold were cast as one piece to preheat the fuel-air mixture, but preheating didn't atomize the gas as well as hoped. The new manifold was only used for five years and only on the Model W. The engine drove a new three-speed sliding-gear transmission.

Opposite: In July 1919, Jack Fletcher rode his Sport Twin to the top of Mount San Antonio, known throughout Southern California as "Mount Baldy," in the background at left. Of course, for the July run, the top of the 10,114-foot mountain was clear of its winter snow and cloud covering.

A number of endurance runs and trials promoted the new model. Among the most esoteric was one reported by Harry Sucher that involved a 1,200-mile survey run through Death Valley. Edwin Hogg was hired by Pacific Coast Borax Company and two railroads that were actually interested in establishing resort hotels and rail lines through the beautiful but intolerant landscape. Hogg completed his travels without any trouble (and eventually a couple of resorts were built). And Harley-Davidson promoted Hogg's travels and his bike's reliability.

Yet another effort quieted the skeptics who had doubts about the abilities of such a lightweight motorcycle. Jack Fletcher took the bike on a hill climb. The hill was Southern California's Mount San Antonio, "Old Baldy," and the climb was a 7.5-mile burro trail to the 10,114-foot summit. On July 9, 1919, Harley-Davidson became the first motorized vehicle of any kind to climb Old Baldy.

Harley-Davidson had expanded its Juneau Avenue factory to nearly 600,000 square feet, and now it had the capacity to produce about 35,000 motorcycles a year. But in 1921, they shipped only 11,000. Sales of the Sport Twin were weak; the bulk of production went to Europe.

Above: Although it was introduced in 1919, the Model W Sport Twin was not even illustrated in company catalogs until 1920. The rest of the production continued on from 1918 and as the war took resources worldwide, one of Harley's economies was to adapt and reuse the 1918 printed matter for 1919. The Model W was powered by a horizontally opposed side-valve twin-cylinder engine with a bore and stroke of 2.75x3.00 inches, for a displacement of 35.64 cubic inches. Unlike other Harley-Davidson twins, which had a separate engine and transmission, the Sport twin had the engine and transmission mounted in the same cases, making the Model W the first Harley-Davidson twins with unit construction. Model W production ended after the 1932 season, and Harley-Davidson would not make another unit twin until 1952, when the Model K was introduced.

Opposite: The Sport Twins offered an external-front-spring suspension for the first time on a Harley-Davidson. Handlebars were one piece of one-inch tubular steel welded into the tube. The seat was still the Ful-Floteing variety. The beautiful decal was standard and unique to these 1919 W Sport Twin models.

Above: Tires were 3.00x26-inch models offered from Firestone, B.F. Goodrich, or Goodyear. The rear brake was getting more sophisticated; it incorporated a band outside the drum to pull tightly on it.

Right: The main drive chains were completely enclosed in sheet metal. This kept the oil in and the dirt and dust out. Harley's Model W never proved popular in the United States. Its different engine and sound never caught on. However, sales in Europe were very good.

The W Sport Twin was dropped from production in 1923, taking with it engineering improvements like side valves, wet clutches, unit construction, and trailing-link front forks. Side valves would reappear soon, but some of the Sport Twin's other features would not return on a Harley for decades.

Automobile sales had much to do with this. Henry Ford had refined mass production and his assembly line techniques to a fine art. He could sell his Model T for $400 to anyone who arrived at his factory in Dearborn, roughly the cost of a sidecar-equipped Harley-Davidson Model J. Chevrolet was ready to introduce a new car to sell at $425. For comparable cost, a family man could carry his entire family, comfortably protected from the weather, on four wheels instead of three.

The market was changing. The postwar economy was growing and so were families. Motorcycles had been known for their economy but they were replaced by automobiles known for their practicality. And with the continuing public interest in motorcycle racing, the roads—many more now paved as streets— were seeing higher-performance, higher-cost bikes available.

H. W. Parsons in his magazine *Motorcycle and Bicycle Illustrated* was the first to point out the new trend. Quoted in Harry Sucher's book, Parsons observed that the motorcycle was no longer strictly necessary as basic transportation. Instead, it was becoming the "toy of the wealthy sportsman," an "expensive form of entertainment."

Hap Scherer, a newly appointed publicity manager for Harley-Davidson, followed in the footsteps of Arthur Davidson in seizing another opportunity. Scherer began to devote a great deal of each issue of *The Enthusiast* to articles on the Sport Twin. He emphasized its broad appeal as low-cost, reliable transportation. He promoted its suitability for touring as well as utilitarian riding and boasted that it was easily manageable by new, young riders and women.

The roaring twenties opened with a bang as retired U.S. Army officer John Thompson obtained a patent for his submachine gun,

unemployment insurance appeared in Great Britain, and in Munich, Adolf Hitler announced his 25-point program.

In 1921, Pittsburgh radio station KDKA broadcast the first regular radio programs in the United States, the German Deutschemark fell, beginning rapid inflation, the United States produced 472 million barrels of gasoline, and the Ku Klux Klan became violent and went public. In 1922, the USSR was formed by combining the various Soviet states; insulin was first administered to diabetics; the first of the "Our Gang" serial comedies appeared; and the first successful aircraft carrier landings took place on the deck of the USS *Langley*.

The United States had been the only world power left undamaged by World War I. And—except for inside the offices of the Big Three motorcycle producers—there was optimism everywhere in the air.

Chapter 4
Racing Improves the Breeds—But Not the Sales

Customers continued to race the twins. In endurance races over public roads and on some horseracing tracks, Harley-Davidson motorcycles began to make a name. But customers complained because the factory provided no encouragement, no support.

While Bill Harley worked to develop new transmissions, Bill Ottaway began studying ways to lessen vibration by more careful balancing of the flywheels and crankpin. For 1914, he modified a 61 ci pocket-valve engine fitted with a special cam and modified valve porting. This he installed in a 51-inch wheelbase, 300-pound racing motorcycle. It was known as the Model II-K, and it was meant to be sold—in limited production—to customer-racers.

In 300-mile races in Dodge City, Kansas, and Savannah, Georgia, the Harley-Davidson did not win. But it finished—a respectable third place in Savannah—and so put notice to Excelsior, Henderson, Indian, Thor, Merkel, and Pope that Harley-Davidson was no longer the last-place machine. Under Ottaway's direction, the factory would no longer leave its customers in the dust of all the other manufacturers.

Race-bred improvements trickled down to street machines and spread around on bikes for the dirt and board tracks. The work paid with results. In the inaugural 1914 Venice, California, race, a 300-mile event run through the streets and on and off of a transplanted banked-boards section, Harley racer Otto Walker averaged 68.3 miles per hour to win. On July 4th, back at Dodge City, Walker and his five Harley-Davidson teammates cleaned up when, late in the race, mechanical failures sidelined the Excelsior and Indian riders. Walker won at 79.8 miles per hour.

And in August, on a new board track at Tacoma, Washington, Walker came second by a single wheel-length behind an Indian. A month later, he won on a new board track in suburban Chicago. He rode Bill Ottaway's newly designed eight-valve

Above: Although this factory racer looks like a stock engine, it is the narrow-crankcase engine based on the 1914-and-earlier-style crankcase. These engines—retired from street-production bikes—were produced exclusively for racing through 1915 and 1916. The 1915–1916 IOE racing twins were the predecessors of the eight-valve OHV race engines that would be introduced for 1916. Only a handful of each type was ever produced. This one, probably a 1916-vintage IOE racer, is owned by Daniel Statnekov and was restored by Brad Wilmarth in Petersburg, Virginia.

Opposite: The narrow crankcase cannot normally accommodate the cylinders that use 1915-and-later large-style intake manifolds as well as valves. This engine uses the later-style cylinders that were specially manufactured to fit the narrow case. These engine parts are not interchangeable with stock engines. This was a 61 ci (1000cc) twin.

Above: This is a short-coupled factory race frame that incorporates a shorter fork. The entire bike looks slightly miniaturized next to a stock production street bike. However, both tanks are larger than stock because riders didn't want to have to stop for gas or oil during longer races. A 300-mile race would still require stops but with these tanks, there might be one less stop.

Opposite: Serial numbers are critically important for determining the history of racing engines. While the second M designates it as a 1916, the first M with three digits designates it was a race motor. It is likely this was a "Wrecking Crew" bike from the 1915 Dodge City race, although of course it would have used an M741K designation for example, since the "K" designated 1915.

engine prototype. Averaging 89.1 miles per hour, Walker set a new record for speed on boards.

Board racetracks had been around since 1910. A California automotive engineer, Fred Moskovics, had read about the banked brick speedway being constructed in Indianapolis, and he believed a similar speedway would do well in California. But he'd also seen indoor bicycle racing ovals made of wood. He determined that wood was easier and cheaper to construct and maintain. So at Playa del Rey, a few miles south of where Los Angeles International Airport sits today, Moskovics built his one-mile track. Made of 2x4s and steeply banked—nearly 50 degrees—he called it his "huge wood saucer," because it was perfectly round. Straightaways came later to stretch the circles into ovals.

But the earliest of these ovals weren't right. There was no smooth transition from straight to turn. For motorcycles averaging better than 80 miles per hour—some with their own instability problems even on flat straightaways—these banks were treacherous.

Enter Arthur Pillsbury. Pillsbury knew nothing about board tracks. But among his other business interests, he had studied railroads and he knew of railroad design. Top-heavy steam engines laboring ahead of several dozen freight cars got around corners going up or down hill without toppling over. Railroad designers developed a technique called the Searless Spiral Easement Curve. This was really a series of corners, feathered one into the next to blend the approach to any curve.

Pillsbury built a mile-and-a-quarter board track in Beverly Hills—where the Beverly Hilton Hotel sits today—and racers never complained. Other builders and promoters came to see Pillsbury's track. When they left, they were convinced and converted. East Coast promoter Jack Prince (a motorcycle racer himself) went on to build board racetracks around the United States between 1910 and 1925 as spectator interest grew.

Track racing became successful. Road races were much less so because the events closed public roads throughout the weekends, inconveniencing nonenthusiasts. But the board tracks began to attract huge crowds. (One element that benefited motorcycle—and automobile—racing was the widely known game-fixing scandal discovered in baseball that renamed the most guilty team the "Black Sox.") Part of the attraction was the tracks themselves; banking, all in 2x4s or 1x2s laid on end, ranged from only 15 degrees up to a seemingly vertical 62-degree wall. Some referred to a track like that in St. Louis as a "pie tin" because the banking was so steep and the transition from flat to banking was so abrupt.

To many spectators it seemed impossible that the outcome of a motorcycle race could be fixed. To others, the draw was the gravity-defying banking. What's more, the speeds that winners reached on these banked boards were increasing steadily. And finally, some

fans were drawn by the risk. As early as 1912, racers were dying in crashes on the boards that broke them and their bikes. The board track in Detroit boasted in letters at least eight feet tall that spectators would see racers "Neck and Neck With Death."

A board track in Newark opened July 4th weekend and closed permanently the following mid-September after a crash killed two young racers and five spectators including four young boys peering down at the races through the steep railings. The rear wheel of one of the rider's bikes came off and landed on the fifth spectator with enough force that within a few days, he died of the injuries.

Despite these tragedies, each of the factories recognized the promotional benefits of winning a race not marred by injury or accident. The races were popular—the motordromes often held 15,000 or more spectators—and no manufacturer could afford to miss opportunities for publicity.

Harley-Davidson's new racing engines were the result of more than $25,000 in development costs, countless experiments, and frustrating failures. Finally, Ottaway convinced Walter Davidson to send for Englishman Harry Ricardo to clear up the engine intake and exhaust problems. Ricardo had developed exceptionally efficient cylinder heads. He sailed from England, and after several weeks working with Ottaway and Davidson, Harley's Model 17 racing 8-overhead-valve engine was producing 55 horsepower from the 61 ci twin.

Ottaway became competition manager and worked as hard on his team's preparation as he did on its machines. Physical fitness, proper nutrition, and adequate rest were mandatory. Pit stops were practiced to perfection. Rehearsals were insisted upon. And it paid off the same dividends as Ottaway's insistence on hiring Ricardo to perfect the heads.

The third Dodge City 300-miler, July 11, 1916, saw Harley-Davidson win again. Otto Walker fell sick the morning of the race and the victory went to 19-year-old Harley team member Irving Jahnke, at 79.8 miles per hour. Two weeks later, on a new board track on Long Island, Harley again performed to Ottaway's expectations taking 1st, 2nd, 3rd, 4th, and 6th. An Indian rider snuck into 5th.

For the 1919 season, Bill Ottaway put together a veritable dream team racing on updated 8-valve-engined lightweights. Riders included Otto Walker again. Ottaway added Jim Davis, Ralph Hepburn, Walter Higley, Fred Ludlow, Ray Weishaar, and "Red" Parkhurst. All the efforts of Excelsior and Indian 8-valve riders were inadequate against what came to be known as "The Wrecking Crew."

Parkhurst won a 200-miler in Marion, Indiana; Walker won all three races at Los Angeles' Ascot Speedway in late November, and he won a 100-miler again at Ascot in late January, 1920. Early that next season, Ottaway's new "pocket valve" engines were introduced to replace the more exotic 8-valves. These were a highly developed version of the basic production engine configuration. Arthur Davidson and his colleagues felt this similarity would benefit sales.

During the 1920 season, Harley-Davidson team member Ray Weishaar, who had shown a consistent fondness for animals, adopted a baby pig as his good luck piece and mascot. In late summer, the pig, named "Hog" and wearing a Harley-Davidson vest of its own, brought Weishaar luck and he won the Marion, Indiana, 200-miler with a new record time of 2 hours, 48 minutes. Afterward, Hog took a victory lap and Weishaar toasted the animal, feeding it a soft drink.

Many of the East Coast banked circle tracks closed down after the Newark accident. Then World War I came along to occupy America's imagination and fears. Understandably, though racing continued to attract spectators, dealers and manufacturers began to notice less interest in the showrooms and fewer sales by the end of 1920.

Above: The shape of the engine timing cover with its oversize external racing pump (in black at lower center) is what gives special racing engines the name "banjo." The overhead valves were operated by long external pushrods. This factory racer was restored and is owned by Daniel Statnekov.

Opposite: This is the famous "banjo" two-cam, eight-valve racer. With this engine, Freddie Dixon won a Gold Star at Brooklands Raceway in England by winning the 1000cc Solo Race at 100.10 miles per hour in October 1923. While this was his most memorable race victory, he and this engine—albeit in various other frames—set numerous records. (Douglas H. Davidson—not related to the founding family—had already reached 100 miles per hour on an IOE twin at Brooklands during a special speed trial on April 28, 1921.)

Harley-Davidson began the 1921 racing season with full efforts despite steadily decreasing sales. The "Wrecking Crew" became the first team to win at average speeds of more than 100 miles per hour. On the boards at Fresno, California, in late March, Otto Walker set a lap record of 108.7 miles per hour. A month later, on the Beverly Hills board track, Walker won again, averaging 104.4 miles per hour.

As Harley-Davidson's 1920 motorcycle sales dwindled to 11,000 bikes, company president Walter Davidson could no longer see any commercial victory coming from competition victories. Even after successive wins at Dodge City, the local government there continued to outfit its police department with Indian motorcycles.

At the end of the 1921 competition season, Harley-Davidson abruptly withdrew from factory participation in organized racing. The company had spent $200,000 that year, paying its top riders salaries as high as $20,000 and covering the costs of mechanics, travel, maintenance, and spares for the team and its machines.

The end caught the team unaware. Sent to Phoenix for races at the Arizona State Fair, the riders participated as a team and performed well. But when the race was over, Otto Walker, Weishaar, Ludlow, and the others found the factory had sent only enough money to cover their hotel and meal expenses but no salaries and no allowances even to return them to their homes. (The mechanics were covered because the factory wanted them, their tools, and the motorcycles back.)

It was a sad and embarrassing end to Harley-Davidson's factory racing efforts. The once-glorious and unbeatable Wrecking Crew racers had to borrow money from the local Harley-Davidson dealer to get home. This was because Walter Davidson, feeling betrayed by the business of racing, would not even accept the racers' collect phone calls asking for help or at least for an explanation.

Right: In 1920, Jim Davis, riding a pocket-valve version of the banjo two-cam, like the one just inside the door, won the Dodge City 300-mile race. In 1921, the last year at Dodge City, this eight-valve OHV version won with Ralph Hepburn on board. Propping the door open are well-used front forks from a circa 1928 Harley hillclimber.

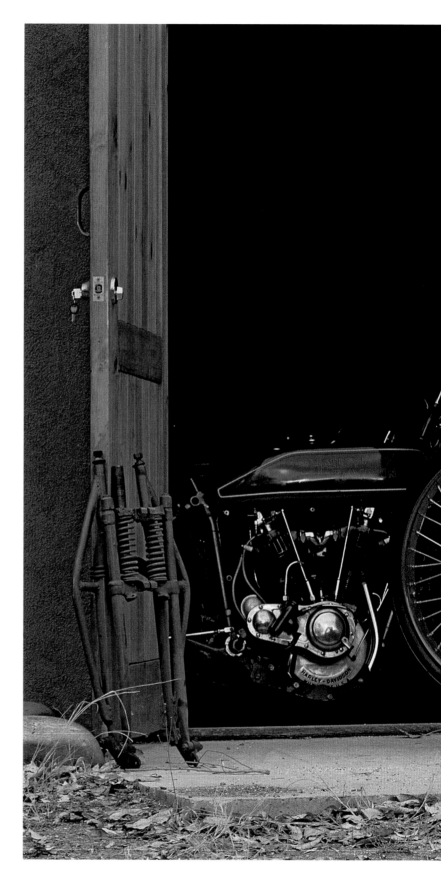

Left Top: Various exhaust port configurations appeared on these eight-valve engines. Sometimes small exhaust pipes were fitted. Early tuners experimented with running both open ports—as shown here—and small exhaust stacks as they experimented with the effects of back pressure on engine performance.

Left Bottom: The serial number 23 8V 1 designates the year of manufacture, that it was the eight-valve rather than the pocket-valve version, and that it was the first one. This racer is one of two surviving banjo eight-valves in existence. Like the 1916 racer, this engine was also fashioned on the narrow-style 1914-and-earlier crankcases. The intake manifold uses a threaded flange to set the distance between cylinders. Lodge racing spark plugs with their own cooling fins ignited the mix.

Right: Feeding the 61 ci OHV racing twin was the 1.25-inch-venturi Schebler Model HX181 carburetor. This carburetor was actually used on 74 ci regular production bikes from 1921 through 1925. The ported air sleeve—the perforated band around the housing near the name Schebler that allows more or less air to mix with the fuel—was decidedly not available on regular production road twins.

Chapter 5
The Finest F-Heads

arley-Davidson was taking it on the chin from Henderson, Excelsior, and Ace. But not at the racetrack. These competitors manufactured four-cylinder motorcycles, and their smooth engines were much more comfortable for police officers spending long days in the saddle. What was worse for Harley, these machines had better acceleration. It was a different kind of road racing, and Harley-Davidson had nothing competitive.

In 1921, the company brought out its updated "Superpower Twin," the 1922 Model JD. With this new F-head engine and its mechanically operated intake valves, the JD introduced Harley-Davidson's big new 74 ci, 18-horsepower twin. The engine used a solid flywheel, which offered the benefit of increased high-end torque while detracting only slightly from acceleration. (The solid flywheel obviously added weight over the previous webbed and spoked-style flywheels.) The JD used a six-volt electrical system that was powered by a storage battery and restored by a generator. The bike sold for $390 at the factory.

No matter. Given their choice, police officers still wanted a four. And in those days, many departments let their officers choose their own mount and then reimbursed them for the costs. So when Ace ran into financial difficulties in late 1924 two years after founder Bill Henderson had died, Harley-Davidson hired its former chief of engineering and design, Everett DeLong. William Harley put DeLong to work on a six-month contract in an off-the-beaten-path section of the company's huge factory. He was assigned to produce a four-cylinder Harley-Davidson.

DeLong first experimented with adapting one of his previous Ace designs. William Davidson vetoed it due to potentially high machine-tooling costs. Then DeLong mounted two J-engines

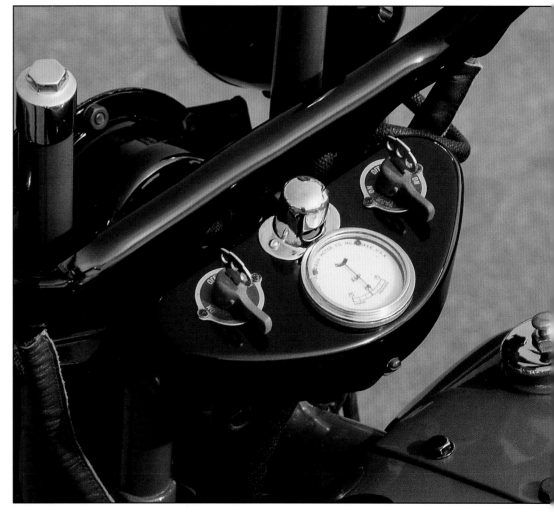

Above: The electrical system consisted of a six-volt generator mounted behind the engine. The generator powered dual headlights as well as the taillight and an instrument panel light for the ammeter. This was the only instrument on Harley-Davidsons for many years. Ignition was by distributor and a high-tension coil, with a circuit breaker fitted into the line.

Opposite: The J-series Big Twin engines—74 ci—were introduced in 1921 and were called the "Superpowered Twin." An electrified version, was available from 1922. But the best of the bunch was the Twin-Cam Model JDH, first offered in 1928 for $370.

Above: The IOE style engine placed the valves in a pocket alongside the cylinder, with the intake valve at the top of the pocket. As Harley-Davidson worked to lower rider position and the gas tanks for more comfort and better balance, the company had to carve out niches in the gas tank for the intake rocker arms to work on the 1928 and 1929 JDH.

Right: By 1928, a front brake was standard equipment. Riders still shifted the three-speed transmission by hand with a foot clutch. Oil was distributed to the engine by a pressurized system regulated by the throttle on the handlebars.

Opposite: Harley-Davidson advertised that the JDH produced 18 horsepower. Bore and stroke were 3.438x4.00 inches. This continued Harley's style of engines with long stroke to produce higher torque. Intake valves were mechanically operated, although cylinders and heads were still one-piece cast iron, nickeled to protect the iron from rust.

side-by-side so that they shared a common crankcase. The cylinders were sleeved in order to reduce their total displacement to only 80 cubic inches.

For reasons not really entirely clear to historians, William Davidson killed the project. Through the years, he had become fanatical about production efficiency and quality control. This pursuit had led him to produce in the Model J, a motorcycle with consistent high quality that could be sold at a good price. Diversity in models worried him because it introduced too many variables to his efficient manufacturing equations. And, because he had become the major stockholder by reinvesting his dividends steadily into the company, his word stuck. The wood mockup was destroyed. Harley-Davidson remained a two-cylinder company. It had, after all, already invested in improvements on its JD that William Davidson had approved.

Nickel protects cast iron and other metals from the elements. It was a common treatment in the first third of the century. The "hurricane" style air cleaner was common on all Harley-Davidson models. It was an early acknowledgement of the damage dust and dirt could do inside carburetors and cylinders.

Introduced in 1924 were Alemite grease fittings on the JD's cases. With the grease gun and can of grease furnished with each new bike, the owner could force the lubrication onto all bearing surfaces (except those within the cylinders) at the twist of a wrist. Another significant development was to replace the old-style cast-iron pistons with aluminum. Because aluminum dissipated heat more efficiently, William Harley believed that the danger of engine seizure from overheated pistons—on long uphill runs, for example—would be greatly reduced with the aluminum pistons.

With no four-cylinder engine to clutter manufacturing facilities and to consume the promotion and advertising budgets, things in Milwaukee returned to business as usual. And "usual" in 1925 meant improving the frame design to lower the seat a full three inches. This allowed additional streamlining that further stretched the teardrop shape of the fuel tanks. Internally, the aluminum pistons weren't quite the success that was hoped. So for 1925, they were replaced with an iron-alloy casting with deeper but narrower piston rings that lessened friction.

The 1920s had begun to roar by the middle of the decade. Duke Ellington and Jelly Roll Morton had their first records by 1926. Al Jolson had sung on screen; movies could talk. Babe Ruth hit 60 home runs, and the first traffic light in America, in Cleveland, Ohio, was already 10 years old. For five years now, drivers in the United States had national highway numbers to direct them to their destinations.

In 1928, Dusenberg had the Model J with 265 horsepower and capable of 116 miles per hour; Ford had its Model A, selling for $450; and Chrysler Corporation took over Dodge and launched the DeSoto and the Plymouth. The big-city streets had flappers in short skirts and men in zoot suits. Violin cases carried submachine guns, speakeasy clubs served booze, and the exploits of Al Capone and John Dillinger and Bonnie Parker and Clyde Barrow were all over the radio and the newsreels.

Scheduled television began in New York and a precise, gentle man in California named Walt Disney introduced Mickey, a talking mouse and his companion, Minnie. American's were singing *Makin' Whoopee* and *Button Up Your Overcoat*, and the Geiger counter was invented to measure something called radiation. While Louis Meyer averaged 99.48 miles per hour in a Miller to win the 1928 Indy 500, on July 4, Leon Duray won at Salem, North Carolina, in a front-wheel-drive Miller, averaging 130.59 miles per hour. The United States was speed—and style—crazy. Society was bubbling, and the economy was bursting.

Into this well-fueled excitement, Harley-Davidson injected its own fire. For 1928, it offered for sale the twin-cam Model JDH Seventy-four for sale for $375. (A JH model Sixty-one was offered as well, for $10 less.) The JDH was the company's answer to customer cries for performance. At $375, the single-seater JDH was never compared with Ford's $450 five-seat Model A; the purchasing motivation was not for transportation. Harley buyers wanted sport.

The JDH engine used two camshafts, one operating intake and exhaust valves for each cylinder, compared to the single cam in the center of the normal J to operate all four valves. This was a system used on the factory racing bikes since 1919. Even more characteristic of current racing technology was the cam action. The pushrods were operated directly. The cams moved tappets which moved the pushrods. This provided quick and more accurate valve response than the previous road-bike systems of rocker arms. The direct-acting valve gear allowed higher engine speeds, producing more horsepower out of the now-27-year-old F-head engines.

The Model JD (Sixty-one) and twin-cam JDH (Seventy-four) engines each u ed magnesium-alloy domed pistons. This increased the compression ratio and further increased power output.

All the J models got front brakes in 1928. Presumably, this arrived as a result of the higher speed capability of the new Two-Cam bikes. But it was a development not so uniformly welcomed. European motorcycles has fitted brakes to the front wheels years earlier; yet the U.S. makers heard no demands from riders for the second brake, and so they waited. Riders in America could more easily imagine skids from applying the front brake too hard—especially on unpaved roads—than they could see the safety advantages of the additional stopping power. In fact, some riders disconnected the front brake cable and grip out of distrust.

Still, Harley-Davidson knew what it was doing and what it had done with this new engine. The company advertised the new JDH as the "Fastest Model Ever" from the Milwaukee maker. Riders could hit 85 miles per hour soon after leaving the showroom. And, after carefully breaking in the engine and removing a little extraneous weight, 100 miles per hour was possible.

And it looked the part. With the lowered profile of the JD models, the gas tanks had to be notched from the bottom

With its tube-shape tool box up front, riders never had trouble staying awake at night. The rattling of tools inside it was louder than the well-muffled engine. This particular 1929 Model JDH appeared in a 1991 Walt Disney film, *The Rocketeer*.

on the right side to accommodate the external rocker arms. This was performance stuff—racing technology—encroaching into practicality. It had appeared on the earlier JD models. But here, the space seemed even more crowded. The look was racier.

The motorcycle as fast, expensive, and exclusive—Harley offered 11 other models in 1928 and 12 others in 1929. It blatantly capitalized on its proven racing heritage. The JDH was directly descended from the Two-Cam racing engines that had first won on the board tracks in Altoona, Pennsylvania. There, on July 4, 1925, ridden by none other than the already-legendary Joe Petrali, a Two-Cam Harley-Davidson averaged 100.367 miles per hour. And for only $375, any wealthy young rider in America could be like Joe.

Chapter 6
The First F-Heads

It seems that it could only be coincidence, American exuberance came to an end on Friday, October 29, 1929. It took hours and days and weeks for the full impact to drift across the continent. Despite the desperation that drove stock brokers to leap from their Wall Street windows before the end of the day, the real impact of the Crash was felt more slowly—if no less painfully—around the country.

Engineering development is a time-consuming process. From the idea to its introduction to the public, time passes in a pace that counts in calendars not hours. Models produced by manufacturers are scheduled for removal from the market months in advance of the actual date it will happen. Still, it could only have been coincidence.

Harley-Davidson's highest performance motorcycle yet, the JDH, was removed from the product line-up at the end of 1929. The Roaring Twenties were silenced as fortunes were lost and the luxuries of high-performance single-seat fashion accessories became insupportable and politically incorrect. The fastest bike yet was—surely it was only coincidence—replaced by a line of slower, more practical, quieter, and more frugal machines: the side-valve V series.

Worse yet, the VLs were just not very good motorcycles at first.

These machines used a new valve configuration and new heads. This improvement allowed Harley-Davidson to lower the motorcycle even more without having inserts cut into the tanks to accommodate IOE mechanisms. These new engines had side valves and were known as "flatheads."

This new Seventy-four was introduced to dealers in August 1929. It was massive, weighing nearly 100 pounds more than the hot rod JDH. Its new, heavier, stronger frame and front forks took the bike up to 530 pounds, ready to ride. Yet the

Above: The 74 ci engine dimensions were unchanged from the standard Model J. The biggest differences to the engine were side valves and removable heads. The Schebler carburetor was standard on Harleys for many years.

Opposite: Harley-Davidson called the Model V, introduced in 1930, its "greatest achievement in motorcycle history." The biggest news was the introduction of removable cast-iron heads on the Model V engine. At the factory, the standard Model V sold for $340; for no extra cost one could buy the VL with the better-performing, higher-compression engine.

True, they got a heavier, stronger duplex chain. Axle removal to change a tire was now down to loosening a single nut on either front or rear axles. Tire widths, growing steadily over the past 15 years, had reached 27x3.85 inches as an option on the JDH. Now 19x4.00 inches was standard on the VL. But it was the engine that took the heat.

As Jerry Hatfield has pointed out the facts in his *Inside Harley-Davidson: An Engineering History of the Motor Company from F-heads to Knuckleheads 1903–1945*, Harley-Davidson had two ways to go when it decided to replace the aging IOE engines. Some European motorcycle makers were using overhead valves, refining the technology and obtaining impressive performance and reliability from an otherwise noisy, complicated set of machinery. At the same time, Indian had virtually perfected the side-valve head and the models with those heads were showing their tails to Harley bikes on the tracks and on the streets. Racing was still important in the United States but even by the late 1920s, the most important speed trials going on in America were the impromptu ones against the Indians that began when any traffic light turned green.

Harley-Davidson adopted side valves.

For reasons never completely understood, the same 74 ci engine that had been the JD, was not quite the same engine in the VL Seventy-four. A new lightweight flywheel allowed rapid acceleration to 50 miles per hour, thereby addressing one of the concerns of police riders and street racers. But the same light flywheel ran out of energy at higher speeds. Power and acceleration faded dramatically. Also, above 50 miles per hour, the imbalances inherent in two-cylinder engines with 45-degree V-angles were not managed by a heavy flywheel. The bike began to shake in ways that historian Harry Sucher described as "teeth loosening and wrist shattering." Clearly an unpleasant experience.

It was so unpleasant that Harley-Davidson lost hundreds of potential police sales after departments tested the bikes and found them wanting and unwanted. The factory began a hasty—make that frantic—redesign program and put into

power output hadn't grown enough to give the new machine the performance of even the previous basic J models.

The biggest change was replacing the previous IOE configuration with its side-valve combustion chamber. Now Harley offered side-mounted valves similar to what Indian had run for years. But whether it suffered from insufficient testing and development or it was just another victim of all the circumstances surrounding the stock market crash, the new VL was a disaster.

Historian David Wright learned from William H. Davidson (sound of founder William A.) that the frames broke, the flywheel was too small, the mufflers clogged with carbon (strangling the engine), and the clutch wasn't up to the additional weight of the motorcycle when combined with the too-light flywheel. The bikes, offered as standard Model V, the VL with higher compression, the VS for use with sidecars, and the VC for use with commercial package cars, all sold for $340. In August, a number of owners enthusiastically traded their JDs for the newest Harley. They were quickly disappointed.

effect a kind of early-day recall. A replacement heavier flywheel was unfortunately also larger, and it necessitated a new crankcase that would not fit into the existing frame, which had to be modified by replacing the bottom frame loop. In addition, the factory changed valve and cam action. All the pieces were shipped to the dealers who were told to contact customers and replace the parts at no charge. Experienced mechanics could accomplish two changeovers a day. But the factory made no offer to pay the dealers for

their mechanic's time, and some of the dealers refused to do the work without pay. Harley-Davidson wouldn't bend, so more than a few dealers deserted, switching over to—or in some cases, back to—Indian. In all, more than 1,350 motorcycles had to be significantly modified to change the image of the VL. The damage was done. It led to some of the earliest myths about Harley-Davidson's motorcycles: that last years' models were always the best, and that the JDH engines were the *absolute* best.

Defying Gravity

Sir Edmund Hillary would have understood perfectly. When asked why he had climbed Mount Everest, the dour New Zealander replied without a trace of humor, "Because it was there."

The quiet Italian from San Francisco, Joe Petrali, couldn't have said it better. Petrali had distinguished himself for more than a decade with hundreds of board and dirt track victories, and he had proven nearly unbeatable running up hills.

Motorcyclists had begun climbing hills as soon as motorcycles could make it to the top. Jack Fletcher was not the first to top a hill when he crested Old Baldy on a 1919 W Sport Twin. But at 10,114 feet, his climb may

Hillclimbing is a particularly American form of racing. It has been described as the motorcycle equivalent of the Brahma bull-riding event at the rodeo. Riders know they'll be thrown to the ground. It is first a question of trying to figure out how not to fall off. The next concern is how to get to the top faster than the other one or two climbers who made it there before you.

The rear tire was chained for traction, using drive-chain links attached to standard oval links. These racers had only one speed. Many of them didn't even have oil pumps because they ran for barely 10 or 12 seconds—and that was if they made it to the top. Unlike other forms of racing, these hillclimb racers also had rear brakes. Because what went up also had to come back down. Daniel Statnekov unearthed and owns this bike.

have been the highest. Routine attempts became sort of standardized. Routes straight up the sides of hills ran 200 to as much as 600 feet through a corridor usually 30 feet wide. Lime was dragged up the course in later years to mark the boundaries, and a string at the bottom and top set the official start and finish lines. Riders had a staging area about 30 feet long to get their bikes up to speed before breaking the start string.

If there was a problem, the rider could shut down. After breaking the string, it was an official run.

Hill climbing's popularity grew in the late 1920s. Throughout the early 1930s, movie theaters even included short segments during newsreels of Indian, Excelsior, and Harley-Davidson riders flying up and sometimes falling back down ridiculously steep hills.

Above left: The DAH was Harley-Davidson's professional hillclimb entry beginning in 1930. Nearly all these engines were manufactured and numbered in 1930 for competition in professional Class A events. The company used this same engine for a European road racer, known as the DAB. Harley always kept its eye on the international racing scene as a way to broaden its markets.

Above right: The plunger on top of the bars locked the magneto into an advanced position. The kill switch—the clamp near the end—was often fastened by a leather thong to the wrist of the rider so that when he came off the bike, the engine died. These DAH overhead, two-valves-per-cylinder engines, although different in every respect from anything offered to the public at the time, were the precursors to the OHV production Knuckleheads that were introduced in 1936.

At the time, Harley-Davidson had a small factory effort based on its new DAH competition engine, which was an overhead-valve (OHV) version of its 45 ci (750cc) Model D side-valve engine. The Model D used four cams, each operating its own pushrod to raise open and drop closed an intake and an exhaust valve. These were available to the public as the standard D and as a higher-compression (5.0:1) Model DL that produced about 18.5 horsepower at 4,400 rpm (compared with 30 horsepower for the VL). The long stroke enabled Harley-Davidson to maintain its legendary torque.

Experiments begun in 1929 continued through 1933 on variations for the DAH hillclimber. By 1932, some engines were alcohol-fueled and mounted in a double-downtube frame suspended up front by a trailing-link fork. Earlier versions used a much heavier single-downtube frame and various fork, handlebar, fuel tank, and transmission combinations. The fuel mix was fed to this engine by a Schebler racing carburetor.

Between 1930 and 1932, the company employed two riders for its limited, factory-supported racing program (it had withdrawn completely between 1925 and 1930

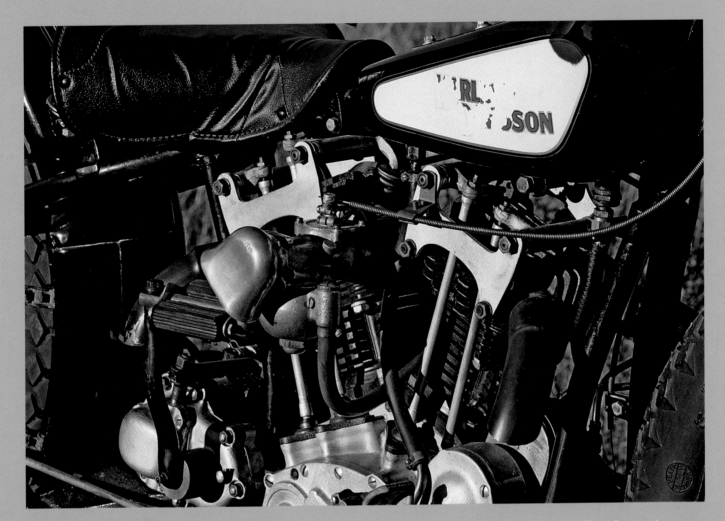

Harley-Davidson experimented from 1929 through 1933 with variations on the DAH hillclimber. This 1932 OHV Forty-five used a double-downtube frame and a trailing-link front fork. Earlier versions used a much heavier single-downtube frame and various forks, handlebars, gas tanks, and even transmissions. This version used the Schebler racing carburetor.

for economic reasons). For 1932, only Joe Petrali remained. He had rejoined the team in 1931. Petrali was an excellent mechanic and an intuitive engineer who had just as often tuned, raced, and won on his own private entries as he had on factory bikes for pay. He developed secrets and techniques that brought him victories on competitors' bikes as well. He consistently scored the highest points in AMA national standings, from 1931 through 1936.

For some time, Petrali campaigned Harley-Davidson's legendary "Peashooter," a quick-revving 21 ci single whose exhaust sounded like a peashooter. When the Model D was introduced, Petrali did not abandon his Peashooter, he just ran more events.

Joe's years of board and dirt-track racing experiences on the agile Peashooter had sharpened his sense of balance. Now, for 1932, Joe had a formidable weapon, the competition DAH. With the extra power

of this alcohol-burner—power directed to the hillside by aggressive rear-tire chains developed from winter ice races—the Harley factory hillclimber was indomitable. Petrali was National Hill Climb champion from 1932 until 1939. (In 1940, the AMA outlawed rear-tire chains and all fuels other than gasoline. The organization wanted to encourage amateurs to compete in hillclimbs through Class C rules.)

When Petrali finally retired from racing, he did not retire from going higher, faster, and farther. He had considerable input into the development of Harley's later engine designs. In March 1936, he took a motorcycle with the new Knucklehead OHV engine to Daytona Beach and set a two-way average speed record for motorcycles of 136.183 miles per hour. And then he went to work for Howard Hughes, developing airplanes. When Hughes piloted his short skip across Long Beach Bay in his eight-engined Spruce Goose wooden airplane in 1947, Joe Petrali was his flight engineer.

Opposite: Tires were 4.00x19-inch inflatable balloons. The rear luggage carrier was a $5.50 option; the rear stand, a Jiffy Stand, was another $3.00. The raccoon tail, not a Harley factory option, was an aftermarket accessory. A total of 1,960 Model Vs were sold in 1930 while nearly twice as many—3,246—buyers opted for the higher-performance VL.

Right: Four gallons of gas and one gallon of oil straddle the top tube. The gear shift was still hand-operated. Harley-Davidson still figured the ammeter was the only instrument the rider needed. Top speed for the Model V was around 75 miles per hour.

Chapter 7
The First Knuckleheads

When the Model E was introduced in 1936, it continued an embarrassing Harley-Davidson tradition. It had problems.

Oil flow had always been a concern in Harley's engines. To be fair, it was troublesome to all engine makers in the first decades of internal combustion. In Harley-Davidson's early F-head engines, the oil lubrication was done by a system called "total loss." The rider filled a reservoir alongside the gas tank and regulated oil flow from the tank by watching drops fall through a sight tube. Normal riding conditions called for three drops every five seconds. This oil worked its way down through the engine and finally dripped through a small tube onto the drive belt pulley shaft and later on to the front chain ring. Harley-Davidson advertised that this system always provided clean oil to the engine and running gear. It was never mentioned that a moderate amount of that oil sprayed onto the rider's leg.

A pump was added in 1911 to give a few extra shots to the engine under heavier strain, when going up hill, for example. The rider's tendency was, when in doubt, better too much oil than too little. Some of that excess oil forced its way past piston rings, clogging valves, fouling spark plugs, and spreading more onto the rider's leg.

With the side-valve engines, an oil pump was linked to the throttle. The more twist of the wrist, the more oil. But it was tricky to regulate, and controlled as it was by a wire linked to the throttle's twist grip, wire stretching affected oiling. Plugs fouled. Engines ran sluggishly until the problems were finally sorted out.

And they always were sorted out. That was a part of the developing mystique of Harley-Davidson. The company always solved its problems. Sometimes these conditions—oiling and others—led plant superintendent William Davidson to literally

Above: The Knucklehead's standard four-speed transmission was still shifted by hand. Four-speed gearboxes were available as a $15 option on the larger-displacement engines (the Seventy-fours and Eighties) until 1937. (It would not be until late 1951 that an optional hand clutch would allow safer getaways from a stop.) Instrumentation included the 100-mile-per-hour speedometer, an oil-pressure gauge with warning window, and the ever-present ammeter.

Opposite: By 1936, Harley-Davidson offered five standard colors with several styles of pinstriping. The 1936 Model E is painted Teak Red with black panels and red rims. The others included Sherwood Green with silver trim, Dusk Gray with Royal Buff trim, Venetian Blue with Croydon Cream trim and also maroon with Nile Green trim.

Harley-Davidson introduced its new "Knucklehead" OHV Sixty-one engine with the 1936 Model E. Only 152 of these were sold in its first year, and only another 126 went out the Milwaukee factory doors in 1937. The E was listed in the order forms as "medium compression" and it sold for $380.

shut down the production line, to ship no more motorcycles until the situations were remedied. This happened in the case of the first production Seventy-four flatheads, the 1930 V-series bikes. All of this led not to a myth but to a suspicion, one that Indian motorcycle dealers did their best to perpetuate: Harley-Davidson may build a good motorcycle but it relies on its customers for development work. The Milwaukee-built bikes always seemed to leave the factory a few months before they were ready, a few thousand miles before they were thoroughly tested, just a short while before all the bugs were completely discovered. And squashed.

The 1936 Model E 61 ci OHV engines continued the legacy. Oil—more accurately, lubrication—was still the problem. In

1934, Harley-Davidson upgraded its oil system by means of a more effective pump. Oil flow to the Harley valves and other parts had been inconsistent; it was either too little or too much but seldom was it just right. The new 1936 OHV engine and its dry-sump, recirculating oil system was a valiant attempt. But this resulted in yet another crisis repair project that saw three versions of oil tanks and lines used in 1936. (Eventually H-D developed a gear-driven centrifugal-valve pump in the recirculating oil system that was introduced in 1941. This new pump incorporated a valve that provided maximum lubrication to the engine at high speed. At low speeds, it directed the oil back to the supply tank, bypassing the gear case.)

The new Sixty-Ones admittedly had outside influences to contend with as well as internal ones. The Depression was at its height. President Franklin Roosevelt's National Recovery Administration strongly recommended that employers hire additional workers rather than incurring overtime among employees already on staff. This was a recommendation that no employer dared to ignore. Harley-Davidson had not enough time and not enough payroll to solve this oil problem in time.

The new OHV engines provided 40 horsepower at 4,800 rpm. The design continued the practice of shortening the stroke in relation to the bore. That allowed the steady increase in power from the F-head engines through the flathead engines to these new OHV engines. The performance improvement that the new engine brought about was necessary to wrest the technical lead from Indian, a company that, while feeling beaten and bruised by 1936, was not yet on the ropes.

The bore-versus-stroke question is important to all engines. For any given displacement, bore and stroke vary in relation to each other, but increasing or decreasing one or the other has dramatic effects on engine performance. Longer stroke engines provide their power at slower speeds, more in the form of torque. Shorter stroke engines achieve their power at higher speeds. They develop less get-away-from-the-stop power but more high road-speed strength. But a shorter stroke gets a bigger cylinder diameter in the tradeoff. That allows room for larger valves to get more fuel in and more exhaust out.

Harley-Davidson's engine uses a split flywheel as a crankshaft. This is designed so that it brings the rear piston up to the top of the cylinder an instant—45 degrees of rotation—ahead of the front. Ignition of these two cylinders is provided by a single coil with a "siamesed" lead to both spark plugs. As a result, the two plugs fire each time that either one is needed. For example, because the rear cylinder has compressed fuel in it when the piston is at top dead center, both plugs spark even though the front is approaching the top of the stroke to expel its exhaust gases.

The explosion powers the rear piston down and brings the front the rest of the way up and back down as it sucks in a fresh fuel mixture. The flywheel brings the pistons back up, compressing the front and emptying the rear. When the front plug is sparked into compressed fuel, the rear piston is already heading down, beginning to suck in fresh fuel.

Slightly odd though this may be, this "phantom firing" was adopted in the earliest days out of a pursuit for simplicity. Unfortunately, this firing system also provided Harley-Davidson with its legendary vibration. Fortunately, it is largely responsible for the exhaust sound that these engines produce.

H-D found itself then in something of a dilemma. The engine could not grow because of the physical limitations imposed within the frame. And it could not turn faster because vibration would get worse. But faster—somehow—was necessary. More American roads were paved, and the competition was making road motorcycles capable of more than 100 miles per hour. So chief of engineering William S. Harley and his staff did what they could. They set out to make the engines breathe better.

Some engine basics should be explained here. Overhead valves—such as those in the first F-heads—offered a big benefit.

The fuel comes pretty much directly into the combustion chamber for ignition. In early Knucklehead engines, however, the valve stems, valve springs, and rocker arms were hung out into the airstream. This was good for cooling, but it was noisy and prone to damage from airborne dirt.

The flathead's side valves solved that one problem while inducing another. Valve lifters inside tubes running alongside the engine raised the intake and exhaust valves into an area on either side of the piston and spark plug. The fuel mixture came up into the head and immediately—and violently—turned 90 degrees to fill the cylinder and then was compressed back into the valve chamber before ignition. At higher engine speeds (say, above 4,000 rpm), side-valve engines would seem to run out of steam. For the rider, this translated to a feeling known as "coming off the cam." In fact, the problem was that the exhaust gases could not be expelled quickly enough because of a reverse shock wave. The incoming fuel air mix met already-combusted

The left side of the engine shows the carburetor intake manifold (the silver tube between the cylinders). The Sixty-one engine had a bore and stroke of 3.31x3.50 inches. The factory claimed 40 horsepower. The angle of the cylinders—45 degrees—was standardized among all Harley-Davidson twin engines.

Off To War, Again

The one ingredient that kills any internal combustion engine is too much heat. Engine designers devote great amounts of thought and time and energy to cooling the engine. More lubrication inside the engine helps. But what works better and faster is getting more coolant to the engine. In Harley-Davidson's case, that meant getting more air around the cylinders.

But what could they do if the bikes were intended for use in locations where the air could be as hot as 120 degrees Fahrenheit? Where the rider might not have the luxury of being able to stop to let the engine cool? Locations and conditions such as one might find in North Africa? During a war?

Get those cylinders farther out into the air.

Stories vary as to how this solution came about. One version has a factory employee dressed as a customer going to New York to look at a BMW motorcycle and coming back with the owner's manual. Another version has one of the founder's sons, William H. Davidson, contacting a Milwaukee dealer whom he knew had a customer with a BMW. And then arranging to borrow the bike and its manual for 24 hours. Yet another records that William S. Harley ordered one through his dealer in Holland and had it shipped to Milwaukee.

Why it happened is more clear. The U.S. Army had given more than a little thought to the motorcycles used by the European Axis nations—meaning, primarily Germany—in their successful raids into Western Europe. It became clear that any improvements on motorized transport and specifically motorcycles that could limit the damaging effects of dirt and weather should be carefully considered. For bikes, telescoping front forks, adequate rear suspension, shaft drive instead of chains, and opposed-twin-cylinder engines made the most sense. In other words, the U.S. Army wanted the BMW R71. So it issued official bid specifications that described a bike like that. Three companies were interested. But how Harley, Indian, or an electric components company named Delco would go about bidding, designing, and building the bikes did not matter to the government. Nor did it matter which of the three companies built it.

Whatever the real story, in late February 1941, William and Walter Davidson and chief of engineering William Harley traveled to Washington, D.C., to negotiate a sales and manufacturing contract on these shaft-drive, opposed-twin, air-cooled motorcycles. The product was coded the XA.

Above: It never appeared in any customer order brochures. Only 1,000 were produced, designed to a specification and built to order by Harley-Davidson. The U.S. Army paid $870 each for them to evaluate their potential as fighting machines for combat use. But by the time the bikes had been passed around the Army test facilities, the battles in Africa—where these might have been best suited—were over. Not a single XA ever saw combat duty.

Opposite: The U.S. Army specified that its contractor build a BMW/R61, and so Harley built the Harley XA. It was a masterpiece of innovation for the Milwaukee maker. It introduced Harley's first foot-shift, hand-clutch combination. The engine, an opposed twin mounted sideways like the BMW, stuck the heads far out into the air for cooling.

The U.S. Army ordered 1,000, paying (according to Jerry Hatfield's research) $870 each for perfect copies of the BMW 45 ci side-valve motorcycles. Like the BMW engine, Harley's XA used a two-throw crankshaft on which both cylinders reacted like mirrors to each other. In addition, the engine crankshaft main bearings were balls rather than rollers. The result was a very smooth, balanced engine. The XAs produced about 23 horsepower at 4,600 rpm with a 5.7:1 compression ration and were frugal to the tune of about 35 miles per gallon.

A wet sump lubricated the engine; this was different from other Harley twins. The cylinders, already set out into the wind stream, were topped with cooling fins sometimes referred to as double-deck. This helped keep cylinder head temperatures nearly 100 degrees cooler than the V-twins, an achievement very desirable for use in hot climates.

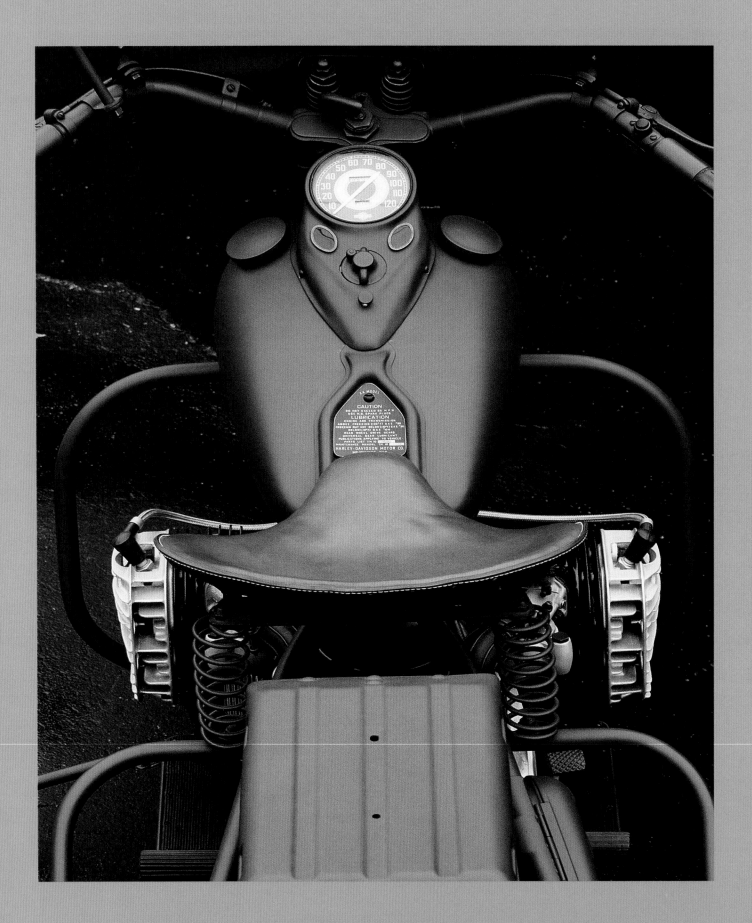

Right: One of the most significant innovations—appropriated from BMW and never used again on a Harley-Davidson—was the shaft drive and final bevel-drive gearbox. The entire concept was meant to be as weatherproof as possible. In addition, the XA was the first production Harley to feature front and rear suspension. It weighed 538 pounds.

Opposite: The XA's wheelbase was 58.75 inches, and it used a 45 ci boxer twin, a flat, opposed two-cylinder with 3.063x3.063-inch bore and stroke, producing 23 horsepower at 4,600 rpm. A Linkert Model M carburetor on each side fed the engine. The fins on the heads are "stacked" fins which allow for even greater cooling.

Below: Pictured with the XA is a 1942 Taylorcraft L-2B, better known as the "Grasshopper." The forward observation plane, complete with invasion stripes, used a Continental four-cylinder A-65-8 boxer engine producing 65 horsepower. Screamin' Eagle, an aircraft broker in Santa Paula, California, with a name appropriate to Harley-Davidson enthusiasts, provided the period-correct aircraft.

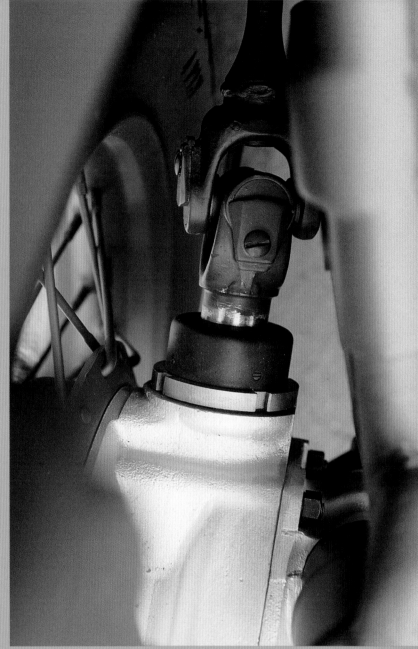

The XAs were fitted with a hand clutch and foot shift, one push down for first, and then three up for the higher gears. Testing over 6,000 miles showed up a few problems but none serious enough to stall the project. As a result, the army began to consider an order of possibly 25,000 of the XA bikes.

Several of the XA prototypes were fitted with sidecars. The rear axle was extended full width to drive the sidecar wheel, but these were only experiments. The army was also looking at a four-wheel utility vehicle proposed by Ford Motor Company in cooperation with Willys Motors.

The first 1,000 bikes were assembled and 800 of those were shipped to Camp Roberts and to the Armored School Motorcycle Department at Fort Knox for additional testing and rider training. In July 1943, the army informed Harley-Davidson that it needed only the 1,000 it had already received. The XA, for all its engineering achievement, never saw battle. Most of its developments were abandoned by Harley-Davidson almost immediately.

Left: Wheelbase had grown to 59.5 inches, and the entire bike weighed 565 pounds without fuel, oil, or rider. The springer front suspension and the spring-suspended rider's seat still offered the only shock absorption on the motorcycles.

Below: The right side of the engine reveals the source of the new Knucklehead's nickname: the valve rocker bosses resembled the shape of a closed fist, fingers down, knuckles up. An internal centrifugal oil pump recirculated oil from the oil tank, through the engine and back to the oil tank, making the Knucklehead the first Harley without a total-loss oil system. The pump included a check valve that bled off oil through the timing case if pressure exceeded 15 pounds per square inch.

Opposite: The "suicide" clutch was actually a modification of Harley-Davidson—and other makers'—standard foot clutches. The standard issue had no return spring on the foot clutch pedal. So, in gear, clutch out at a stoplight, the clutch remained out if the rider needed left foot balance. The modification put a return spring so the pedal lifted like an automobile clutch—with obvious results.

Above: Sidecars provoke two distinct responses. One is from the romantic who envisions the picnic at the end of the ride. The other is from the soloist who dreads picnics at the end of a ride. For both riders, the handling limits of the bike and sidecar are lesser or greater drawbacks.

Opposite: Another option available for the motorcycles was the "Utility Group" for sidecar motorcycles. This included a hydraulic shock absorber for the springer front end, the front safety guard, a steering damper, a front fender lamp, a trip odometer, and 5.00x16-inch tires. It cost $31.50. For $85.00, riders could order the Deluxe Group for sidecars, a package of dress-up parts for the sidecar itself, including a spare wheel, tire, and carrier; sidecar light and wiring; a taillamp on the fender; a chrome fender tip, and a windshield and apron.

Right: A sample of the owner's vision, this heavily chromed FS Seventy-four Big-Twin engine is nearly blinding in the afternoon sun. The Seventy-four version of the Knucklehead was introduced in 1941, and both Sixty-one Model E and Seventy-four Model F Knuckleheads were built through the end of the Knucklehead line in 1947.

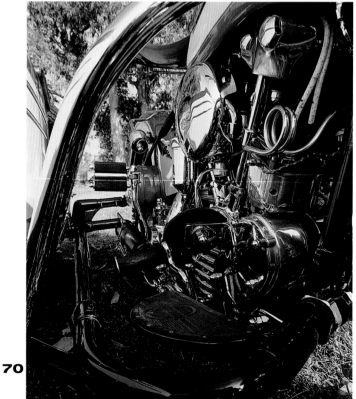

gas that blocked its entrance. Side-valve engines were cheaper to manufacture and quieter (the valves were enclosed within the pushrod tubes) than OHV engines, and because of their simplicity, they needed less frequent maintenance. But they were not efficient.

Overhead valves and bigger valves—something possible only with larger bore cylinders—meant better breathing.

As early as August 1931 Harley and his engineers began to draw and create the Sixty-one OHV twin engine. Contemporary thinking held much as it had in 1903, and Harley saw no reason to enclose rocker arms and valve stems. This was reasonable since most road motorcycles now operated less often on dirt than on pavement.

A year and a half later and about six months before the first prototype OHV turned over, President Roosevelt closed the banks. So President Davidson closed ranks. Factory salaries were cut between 10 and 15 percent and the four founders cut their pay in half. The flathead Model V motorcycles would be dropped for 1935, and all the sales efforts and promotion would go into the new OHV Model E bikes.

Then, in September 1933, the OHV engine first ran. The total loss oil system was back. Unintentionally, the engines leaked.

William H. Davidson, plant superintendent William A.'s son, learned that testing was nearly complete by late August. He recommended that Harley-Davidson use its new OHV motorcycle to wrestle some speed records from Indian. But the board, wary of all the problems so far, advised waiting until the Model E was fault-free. A failure to achieve a new record due to any kind of engine problem would be disastrous.

The heads of these new bikes featured only minimal coverage of the rocker arms. One of the problems the factory had to solve was the one soaking the inside of test riders' legs with oil. The new covering enclosed the right ends of the rocker shaft atop the cylinder.

In mid-December 1935, at last, series production began on the Model E, and the first of the planned 1,600 bikes rolled out the door. But the oiling problems continued even into production. It wasn't until early 1937 that the speed records were attempted.

A Pasadena, California, motorcycle police officer, Fred Ham, took his carefully-broken-in Model E to Muroc Dry Lake (now

If romance was your destination and style was your vehicle, you might even over-restore your 1947 Model FS, adding Croydon Cream panels to the Flight Red body and chroming a few more pieces than the factory would have. Between 1936 and 1946, the sidecars were made by the Abresh Body Shop. After that, Harley-Davidson took the work in-house even as the market began to shrink.

known as Edwards Air Force Base) in Southern California's 2,680-foot-elevation high desert. On a five-mile circle outlined with flags for daylight and flare pots for night riding, Ham rode for 24 hours beginning April 8th and finishing April 9, 1937. He stopped only for fuel, oil, fruit juice, and to change a broken rear chain during the 20th hour. Ham covered 1,825 miles, averaging 76.02 miles per hour for the entire 24 hours, and set 43 new speed and distance records for himself and Harley-Davidson's brand-new Model E.

But still the oil leaked. Through the production of 1936 and 1937, H-D fitted an individual cup and cover for each valve.

Then, in 1938 Harley fully enclosed all the valve gear in black-painted steel behind those shiny covers. With this improvement, the mystique of Harley-Davidson and these new motorcycles was set for its next step. The process had begun with exploits like Fred Ham's 24 hours in the saddle. The mystique would spark to life around 1948 when, so the story goes, a nickname was coined to distinguish this engine from its successor. When the 1936 Model E and the later ELs were viewed from the side, the aluminum housing that covered the ends of the rocker arm shafts formed the shape of a closed fist with the fingers down and the knuckles up.

The Seventy-four came about because customers wanted "a model that would handle a sidecar with ease and speed ..." With their standard springer front suspensions, the FS (with sidecar gearing and medium compression) sold for $605. The sidecar Model 47-LE was another $172.50.

Nineteen forty-seven was the last year of the Knucklehead engine. Only 401 of the sidecar-geared bikes were sold that year. F-engine production began in 1941 and was lumped into wartime production materiel allotments. Still, throughout its life, the FS was an exclusive market. Only 1,302 sold out of total production of more than 160,000 civilian motorcycles since 1903.

Chapter 8
Home From the War Again and off to Hollister

Motorcycles had played a role in the military since General Black Jack Pershing included some of them on his forays into Mexico to chase the outlaw Mexican General Pancho Villa. In Europe and throughout Asia, each armored division contained 540 of the company's Model WLAs. In fact, between 1941 and 1945, Harley-Davidson produced some 88,000 motorcycles for U.S. and Canadian forces for World War II uses. That put a long of young men on motorcycles and gave them plenty of seat time.

When these men came home, many of them returned only with the skills they'd acquired in the army. They could make war, fix motorcycles, and ride them well. When they enlisted or were drafted, they—like their sons 25 years later and their fathers 25 years before—were assured they'd be home by Christmas and that they'd come home as heroes. Four years later when they did get back, the country was grateful, but there were no jobs. War-based industries, swelled by wartime economies, were struggling from overcapacity and underutilization. They had little to do and few prospects for much more to occupy their time. Many of these young men took what remained of their war pay and bought war surplus. With no more money than what lingered in their pockets, they could still afford motorcycles—war surplus WLAs were everywhere—and with no families, they didn't need cars. They came together in small groups and compared horror stories of how it was over there and how it is back at home. And they worked on their bikes. And understandably, these men became bitter and restless once the brief heroes' welcome had worn off.

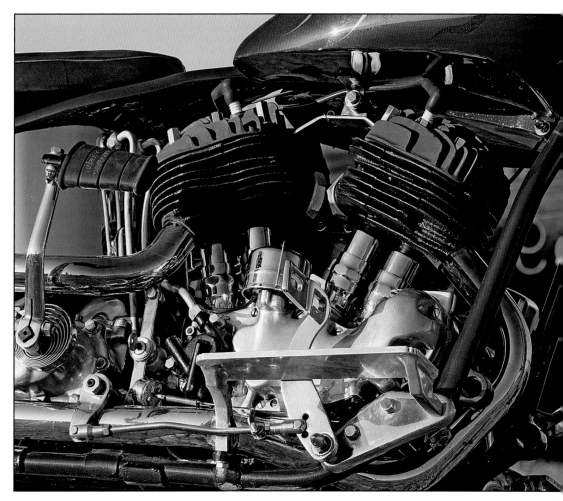

Above: Not all that glitters is chrome. In fact, on this bike little of it is chrome. Much is hand-polished aluminum. When he rides, Mendez says he hangs his toes off the boards. When he scrapes his shoes, he knows he is leaned over too far.

Opposite: Andy Mendez, who owns a shop named Top Dead Center, spent eight months producing this side-valve low rider between paying-customer jobs. He fitted a 1930 Model VL front end and raked the steering neck. He fabricated the pipes and created the fuel tank by welding two tanks together.

This 1940 flathead custom doesn't just look low. It is low. That's only 23 inches to the seat, 35 inches to the top of the bars. It sits on a 63-inch wheelbase. Owner-builder Andy Mendez says of his custom low rider that when they're this low, they keep him out of trouble.

The American Motorcycle Association resurrected its Gypsy Tour, a roaming race series begun before the war that sanctioned competitions around flat tracks and up steep hills. The new Gypsy Tour sites became destinations for the groups of jobless, disappointed, dissatisfied men. They rode with the careless abandon of people who had seen much worse and had nothing left to fear or to live for. In ever increasing numbers, they formed clubs, and their clubs joined others, and they headed for the races. There, among vast numbers of their own, they could watch riders move with even greater abandon. They could at last see something they could respect and admire.

Gasoline as cheap and so was beer. Hotels were sparse in the countryside, and motels just weren't around yet. So when hundreds of racing enthusiasts rode into town, there were never enough places for them to sleep, eat, and care for themselves, even with the best civic preparation.

The Gypsy Tour had a scheduled stop in Hollister, California, on the Fourth of July weekend in 1947. Hollister was a modest but self-confident town of 4,000. The area business people, housewives, and farmers had already made the town known for being America's major garlic producer. At the Veterans Park on the southeast outskirts of town, the AMA had sanctioned track races on the banked dirt 1/3-mile oval.

The first wave of riders washed into Hollister Friday, and by nightfall, hundreds of riders were blowing off steam. By Saturday, the visiting crowd had swollen to perhaps 4,000 riders and companions—almost exactly the resident population of the area—from four states. The small police force was overwhelmed, and they called in the California Highway Patrol and the Monterey County Sheriff. The day's sanctioned racing was finished, but sunset in central California in July holds on until about 9:00 P.M. Young riders were showing off, racing on two wheels side by side and alone up and down Main Street past a bar called Johnnies, which had become a kind of headquarters for a group of riders from Oakland known as the Booze Fighters.

The highway patrol rolled into town with an open-deck semi trailer loaded with a band. This group was quickly hired because they could be loud and they had a reputation for playing music people could dance to.

The 358th: Hell's First Angels

Consider this once more. Between 1941 and 1945, Harley-Davidson manufactured about 88,000 military motorcycles during World War II. In a single year, 1943, aircraft manufacturers in the United States turned out 90,000 war planes. While Harley-Davidson used code letters to name its bikes, the aircraft manufacturers recognized the value of propaganda—and poetry. So Boeing, Douglas, and Lockheed called their B-17s the Flying Fortresses. Consolidated called its B-24s the Liberators. Plans were named Helldivers, Lightnings, Thunderbolts, and Warhawks. And the flight crews and their ground support teams nicknamed these war birds, honoring girls back home and places far away and things that meant a lot and things that never were but maybe only come out during wars. The flight crews and ground crews named them *Memphis Belle*, *Yardbird* and *War Bride*, *Vicious Virgin* and *Dauntless Dotty* and *Princess Pat* and *Sweet Pea* and *Queen of Hearts* and *Jamaica Ginger* and *Belle of the Brawl*.

Based in the English Midlands at Molesworth near Melton Mowbray, B-17 Flying Fortresses were attached to the 358th Squadron of the 303rd Bombardment Group of the U.S. Eighth Army Air Force. One of the 10-man combat flight crews completed 48 successful bombing missions—at least 47 without ever turning back. It was an incredible record. Other Eighth Air Force B-17s had completed as many as 50 missions before, but none had flown as many combat missions without having to turn back with mechanical difficulties. That was because her (and bombers were always feminine) six-man ground crew worked maniacally, often 24 hours straight, to keep the plane flight—and combat—worthy. She flew, loaded like a flying boxcar, laboring like all the B-17s, over the Netherlands, France, Belgium, and into and out of Germany surrounded by artillery and aircraft that didn't want her there. She was the visitor no one wanted. She came, she saw, she destroyed.

She often came home riddled with holes from flak. In the course of 48 missions, she consumed 3 landing gears, 5 sets of brakes, 9 tires, 16 engines, and more superchargers and oil-cooling systems than any of the ground crew counted. She never came home without her crew alive and intact. There were no Purple Hearts awarded to this combat crew of the 358th.

She flew home to Tinker, Oklahoma, on January 20, 1944, where she had been built, to a heroes' welcome. In her honor, the entire 303rd Bomb Group left behind at Melton Mowbray renamed themselves after her. By January 9, 1945, the 303rd had completed 300 successful missions flying under the group name. More than 20,000 tons of bombs were dropped, most of them during daylight bombing raids. The original bomber was one of the first to tempt that fate, flying brazenly into the early morning face of Hitler's *Luftwaffe*.

When the planes arrived from the States, they were painted only in military trim. There were four flight units at Molesworth plus a hangar squadron for major repairs—the 358th, 359th, 360th, and 427th—and each squadron usually included a crewman with artistic talents who would, for the price of a few drinks, paint nose art on the planes or onto the backs of flight jackets. There was a great deal of debate and argument between the men over the name that would emblazon their plane. Combat and grounds crews in the 358th came from California and Oklahoma and when the ladders were removed, a short figure on roller skates holding a bomb pointed down was painted on both sides of the cockpit, and *Hell's Angels* was the name they'd chosen.

No one today knows where the name came from or what it meant to the 16 men who finally agreed on it. Wherever it originated, its name was rich with connotations. It had first appeared on the silver screen as the title of a World War I aviation war film produced by Howard Hughes in 1930. But the dialog made no reference in the film to its title.

Coincidentally, a bombardment technician who was stationed with the 303rd at Molesworth, Edwin Deegan, could quickly recall only a single motorcycle on the base. Whenever the squadron got a six-hour pass, the motorcycle's owner, a handsome fellow from California, would fire it up and head into nearby Peterborough for a couple of beers just as the stars of the Hughes' film had done. Deegan couldn't recall the make of the motorcycle, but he remembered the rider. The fellow flew six or eight missions as an armament officer in the 358th, and Deegan would have fitted the bombs to his plane. The motorcyclist cut quite a figure, especially on his motorcycle, wrapped in a big parka, wolf fur surrounding his face, blown back by the wind. But after those few flights, he was sent home. Deegan figured the government had something else in mind for him, and he imagined that a number of powerful interests thought this fellow's time might be better spent in propaganda. So he worked in films. Deegan saw him often, years later, but always on the screen. His name was Clark Gable.

Five years later, in 1950 in Fontana, California, about 30 miles east of Los Angeles, a group of angry young men who also rode motorcycles were casting about for an identity. These were individuals for whom the American dream of marriage and home and mortgage and calm held little appeal. The adrenaline rush of war had not completely left them, and suburbia was not the same as the back roads and fields and seaports of France and Belgium and England. Among the most mythical of World War II warriors were the Hell's Angels bombers, fliers who wreaked the most havoc, left the most destruction in their wake, thunderers whose four air-cooled 12-cylinder radial engines sent fear down to the listeners below.

The bomber group was born in California. It took its first flight training at Muroc Lake, the same place where five years earlier, Pasadena patrol officer Fred Ham had circled the lake 365 times on a 24-hour motorcycle run. The flight crew and the ground crew were boys flush with military pay and isolated from urban temptations. They bought motorcycles, Harley-Davidsons and Indians, and roared around the lake and the desert and into the nearby town of Mojave. Full of energy and anticipation and anxiety, the boys of Muroc let off steam on motorcycles. Somewhere in the back of at least one of their minds, they already had a name. They would call themselves Hell's Angels.

It was the perfect name for the kind of low-altitude warfare that was in the minds of the boys of Fontana.

Mendez used a 1940 high-compression Model ULH 80 ci flathead engine, the fourth of five years of the biggest flathead twin production. Bore and stroke were 3.42x4.25 inches. When the flathead Eighty was replaced, it was by the F-series Seventy-four OHVs. The Eighty twin would not return until the 1978 model year.

The band and its mobile bandstand were parked between Fifth and Sixth Streets on a broad open boulevard several blocks away from Main. Then the highway patrol began to herd the motorcyclists and their girlfriends over to the music. Most of them went peacefully, but as one assessment put it, about 1 percent, just about 50 people, were arrested, most for drunkenness, but some were hauled in for resisting arrest or indecent exposure.

But 50 arrests in a small town in central California is big news on a slow holiday weekend to the night city editor of a major metropolitan newspaper 150 miles away. On most papers, the experienced staff knows to put in for days off on long holiday weekends. So the city editors and news reporters and photographers who work these weekends are often a little less experienced, their judgment a little less seasoned. And they are a little more willing to work hard to chase a story, to create a reputation as hard-driving journalists even when they've already missed what really happened.

The San Francisco *Chronicle*, on a telephone tip from a Monterey Sheriff dispatcher, sent a reporter and photographer by chartered airplane out to Hollister to "get the story." By the time they arrived, the "story" was over, through the streets still wore the litter of hundreds of beer bottles.

Small-town America, eager for what pop-culturist Andy Warhol would later call everyone's 15 minutes of fame, told the big city reporter what it thought he wanted to hear. And the photographer, arriving with the reporter long after the pictures had been there to take, had instead to find a picture to make.

A round young man, eyes drooping to slits, was posed on a Harley-Davidson Knucklehead parked in front of Johnnies Bar. A beer was placed in each hand, something to which he probably had few objections. A few more empties were kicked into the foreground beneath his feet. The flash bulb plastered shadows against the wall, the photographer reloaded his camera, made another exposure with another blast of light and they were gone. Deadlines to be met, paper to put out, ya know. Gotta go, see ya. Bye.

The next morning headlines struck fear into the hearts of San Franciscans. The small town that some of them knew because of its garlic had been invaded (not exactly) by a band of 4,000 young marauders (not really). Girls had been carried off (not true). Motorcycles were ridden into bars (true). Generally riotous behavior had terrorized the entire town for hours (false). Young men and women had slept in the parks and nearby orchards (true) and had even relieved themselves into the gutters (true; Porta-Potties hadn't been invented yet).

But in Hollister, clocks ticked slowly. Its 15 minutes of fame wasn't over yet.

The wire services routinely pick up from local newspapers stories and photos what may be of national or international interest. The photo of the biker-boozer, one of the hoard that held Hollister hostage, was transmitted nationwide. An alert night picture editor on staff at *Life* magazine saw the photo and saw the possibilities.

Life magazine was sold mostly on the news stands. It had to compete with *Look*, *Colliers*, and *Saturday Evening Post* for the readers' quarters. This photo cried out for cover display. The story, instead, would hold it. Thousands of unruly motorcycles! Arrests! Riots! Girls! Destruction! It was news! And the picture editor offered it to the managing editor who bought it, hook, line, and sinker.

Right: The rear fender came off the front and was skirted. Mendez builds his bikes—and his customer's engines—not only for appearance but for performance as well. This long low rider gets regular exercise chasing the sunset or cruising to Malibu to visit The Rock Store on Sunday.

Below: The 1980 FXWG was Harley-Davidson's first factory "chopper." It was created by Willie G. Davidson, grandson of the founder, after a walk through the parts department and countless conversations with customers. It was his homage to the riotous heritage of Harley-Davidson, heritage that was founded at Hollister, California, on the Fourth of July weekend, 1947.

Opposite: By 1980, the embarrassing behavior that had characterized outlaw motorcycle gangs in the late 1940s and 1950s had been accepted by the company as part of its history. Flame paint jobs and extended front forks were no longer chopper shop modifications. This bike was a Milwaukee factory custom.

Above: The banking is all that remains at Hollister's Veterans Park today. The American Motorcycle Association Gypsy Tour raced there before and immediately after World War II. Access to the infield of the one-third-mile modified oval was through the tunnel at the north end of the track.

Above: The Hollister banked oval races went on for years after the Fourth of July riots. In the end, the area became built up, surrounded by residences. Attendance dropped, and racer interest waned. Finally a local minister began to complain about the noise, and the races were canceled. The infield now contains three baseball diamonds.

Opposite: The FXWG–the WG stands for Wide Glide, so named because of the wide-spaced forks and ultraskinny 21-inch front wheel and tire–used the 80 ci Big-Twin engine. Bore and stroke are 3.50x4.25 inches, with an estimated 65 horsepower. It was an immensely popular experiment on Willie G.'s part: 6,085 sold in its first year.

In the days before direct-dial, long distance, and faxes, and CNN, there was no way for the *Life* staff to verify the story that the wire services picked up from the *Chronicle*. And in those days, the *Life* magazine presses ran late Sunday night

Stop the presses, tear out the front page!

Within a week, everyone on a motorcycle was an Oakland Booze Fighter, overweight and bleary-eyed and coming to get everyone else's innocent, beautiful daughter.

The noise of big motorcycles that was merely loud and perhaps intrusive until that Fourth of July weekend became frightening, like the air raid sirens of the past half decade. The twin-cylinder echo meant that trouble was on the way. These people were bad—very bad—and they didn't care.

A year later when the Gypsy Tour returned to Hollister, fewer than 2,000 spectators showed up on bikes. The highway patrol reported that there were no problems in town. Three drunk drivers were arrested and 65 other traffic citations were issued—all to passenger cars driving on U.S. Highway 101, a dozen miles west of town.

The races had begun in Hollister before World War II. They continued after 1947 until the early 1960s when attendance had fallen off to the extent that it was no longer economically viable for the city to host them. Finally, a local minister began making noise about the noise the motorcycles made.

The track was abandoned, let go to weed. In the infield where teams and VIPs and racer-wannabees had stood watching the races, where about 1 percent of the 4,000 contemplated other things to do during the night ahead, baseball diamonds were laid out. And Veterans Park was overgrown by tidy houses safely set down behind tall, thick masonry walls.

The myth was in place.

Chapter 9
Return to Racing

Back in 1929, after the usual gestation period, a new group of engines were born and christened the D series. These were 45 ci flathead twins. They (and the flathead Model Vs) were a spurt of family growth that was planned long before the hardships of the Depression tightened everyone's belts.

The series was offered from the start in the standard D and the higher-compression DL. The DS with sidecar gearing was introduced in 1930, and the higher-compression DLD became available in 1931. All of them used Lynite pistons. In 1932, the D series was heavily revised and renamed the R series—R, RL, RLD, and RS—and the new Forty-fives maintained Harley-Davidson's reputation for competitive prowess.

The Depression slowed development. Buyers carefully husbanded their limited (or non-existent) resources. That left smaller funds to manufacturers like H-D to improve the breed or to replace aging products. Still, work continued and in 1937, the model year after the Knucklehead was at last introduced, the R-series bikes changed names once more.

The change, to W-series designation, was mainly because these Forty-fives got their own version of Harley's new dry-sump recirculating oil system. The W series included the W, WL, and WLD. The factory offered the WLD in a racing version—with an R tagged on the back end.

William Harley's three-speed transmission was fitted to the road-going Ws, but it was not a perfect match. There was a gap in gearing between second and third, which meant that riders had to wind the engine up tight before upshifting to third. Otherwise, the engine would lug at the bottom end of its power until engine speed crept up.

Above: At the hands of a good "tuner"–a team mechanic/ wizard–the WRs put out about 30 horsepower. On a bike weighing 300 pounds without rider, that power was good for 110 miles per hour on one-mile oval tracks. The extra padding on the rear fender was not a buddy seat. It was meant for the racer to slide back to lower his body against the wind.

Opposite: The WR marked the first time Harley-Davidson sold its full-on competition bikes to the public. In 1933, Class C rules said riders must ride the bike to the races, remove the headlights and taillights (and brakes if it was an oval race) and compete. Then reassemble it to ride home. That part of the rules didn't last too long before it was ignored.

Left: In 1941, Harley-Davidson introduced its WR, the racing version of its 45 ci production Model W twin. The racing bike retained production iron barrels but used aluminum alloy heads and a huge Wico magneto for spark. Bore and stroke was 2.75x3.81 inches.

Opposite: In 1933, the AMA inaugurated a new stock racing category, Class C, for production-based motorcycles to encourage independents to join the fray. Harley's R-series bikes of the day and the later W-series bikes, with cast-iron heads and cylinder barrels, three-speed transmission with foot clutch, and hand gear shift and 45 ci side-valve engine, fit the rules.

Below: The premier American motorcycle race for decades has been Daytona. For many of those years, motorcycles (and cars) raced on the wide sandy beach. In those days, Harley-Davidson ruled the American Motorcycle Association, not literally but so figuratively that classes were defined around Harley (and Indian) engine sizes.

Harley-Davidson went on to build tens of thousands of WLAs for the U.S. Army, and it had supplemented the bikes with enough spare parts to assemble thousands more. After the war, surplus WLAs were abundant and sold for little more than scrap-metal prices.

Back in 1937, the AMA had established the new racing category, Class C, for motorcycles "same as you can buy." The goal the motorcycle association had in mind was to get private owners back into competition. Class C racing motorcycles had to begin life as stock machines purchased out the front door of a dealership. The category was limited to 45 ci (750cc) side-valve engines or 30.5 ci (500cc) OHV engines for flat-track and road-racing events. (The engine size regulation favored Harley-Davidson's—and Indian's—side-valve models against English and European OHV higher-performance bikes. It was, after all, a rule written by the American Motorcycle Association, which H-D and Indian owned and manipulated freely for their own gain.) Hill climb events and TT (Tourist Trophy—named after the race run around England's Isle of Man—races involving at least one right turn and at least one jump, a forerunner of motocross) rules allowed Sixty-ones, Seventy-fours, and Eighties.

(Harley had introduced its 80-inch twin in 1935 and even had a 30.5 ci OHV single cylinder that same year, strictly for racing reasons. The Eighties were known as the VLDD Sport Solo and a VDDS low-compression model for sidecar uses. The 30.5, called the Thirty-fifty, was referred to as the Model C.)

Rules initially required competitors to ride their Class C racers to the track, so Harley-Davidson sold their WLDR fully equipped with all road equipment—brakes, headlights, and all. By 1938, the Class C races were the most interesting in racing and hill climbing. Unfortunately, Harley-Davidson finished regularly behind Indian in this hot competition. But the factory continued to support and encourage privateers and parts, and ideas flowed from Milwaukee for the WLDRs.

For 1941, H-D introduced two specifically dedicated motorcycles for racers: the WR and WRTT. Through the late 1930s, racers had gotten more serious about their machines.

New WLDRs may have been delivered through the dealership front door and possibly some were ridden to their first race. But afterward, most never again saw headlights, and many were towed to the events. The rules became slack in some areas. The WRTT was offered without lights and front fender but with front brakes as were needed for road racing. The WR was stripped further of all brakes as these represented were extra weight and were not used in flat-track events. (They were always removed by racers anyway.) These new bikes were given a larger-diameter carburetor, much stronger valve springs, and other tricks and treats. What's more the intake manifold and ports and the combustion chamber were all polished to improve fuel-air flow. The WLDR shared in all these improvements, offering street riders a true high-performance Forty-five for the stoplight races.

But on the track, the new WR was beginning to excite riders and spectators alike. Racers and their tuners were allowed to prepare the bikes. Harley-Davidson published a thick catalog chocked full of performance engine parts, rear wheel sprockets, different-diameter wheels, large and small gas tanks; in short, a kind of wish book for racers. The rules went further, allowing

Above: The WR became basically a kit-bike racer. Because it was based on stick, the owners adjusted the bike to various competitions. Large gas tanks were used on long races like the Daytona 200 over the sand while peanut-sized tanks were the choice for half-mile ovals. Brakes were needed for road races but were illegal for the ovals.

Below: Independent racing meant long days and volunteer help, up before sunrise to load and transport and unload the bikes. The WRs were officially produced through 1951 but a handful, about eight, were built in 1952 for hard-working and successful private entries to keep up the challenge.

owners to go inside the engine, to reshape heads, to modify oiling systems. Tame things like changing gear sets were common practice. In theory, by standardizing the bikes and engines, the first one across the finish line at the end of a 10-lap TT event or a 200-mile flat-track run had won by virtue of better work and superior riding. In fact, it was often a case where the factory's inside tricks and dollars competed against underfunded enthusiastic amateurs.

Racing historian Stephen Wright reported just how serious the AMA got about it. They had suspended Class A category racing in 1938 because of lack of public interest and by then, Class C had become the premier series. In 1949 at their December board meeting, they passed a pair of rules that could be referred to as the great equalizers:

One required that to be eligible for competition in Class C, a manufacturer had to have sold or have available for sale 25 or more of the model entered. The second rule stated that any motorcycle could be claimed—just like at a horse-track claiming race—no more than 30 minutes after the event for a fee of $1,000 cash or certified check.

The first rule kept the manufacturers honest. Prototypes couldn't race. The second rule kept the entrants from investing heavily in exotic one-off specials. Who would risk their bike

The last year for the WR, 1952, was the first year of the KR, a necessary overlap because of so many first-year problems with the new K-series racing engines. The KR flat-tracker with hardtail rear end and KRTT road and TT racer with swingarm rear suspension were the racing versions of the newly introduced Model K road-series bikes that offered hand clutch and foot gear shift, swingarm rear suspension, and telescopic forks.

knowing it could be claimed by anyone—spectator, official, or other competitor—for just $1,000 immediately after the race?

The racetrack was finally leveled, at least at the starting line.

Well, not entirely.

It seems that after World War II, the United States once again emerged as the largely undamaged victors. True, loss of lives and casualties were fearsome. But for the second time, no battles had been pitched within the continental confines. And so, when it came time for peace, President Harry Truman looked around and saw a bruised and bleeding world filled with friends and former foes alike whose real estate and whose economies were destroyed. A huge plan, named after Secretary of the Army George Marshall set out to provide large-scale economic assistance throughout Europe and Japan. Among Other benefits offered to foreign governments and

manufacturers was a reduction to nearly zero of import tariffs on machine and manufactured goods. And because foreign manufacturers needed raw materials such as steel, rubber, and aluminum perhaps even worse than did domestic industries, the home talents were rationed these materials, much like they were during the war. Motorcycles, produced by England especially, but also Italy, Germany, and Japan (who made a respectable copy of the Harley-Davidson VL before, during, and for a short while after the war) were relieved of most of the tariffs from before the war, reducing the costs of import bikes to fractions of Harley-Davidson and Indian prices.

But it didn't matter. The British pound had been devalued giving the English bikes something like a 20 percent price cut. Labor and raw materials costs in Milwaukee had increased Harley's prices to such an extent that the advantage lay with bikes from Europe. What made Class C racing still work was that the AMA rules had been written to allow the new OHV imports to compete albeit with some difficulty. And they came. And they raced, and they won. Triumph, Norton, and BSA all had 500cc OHV bikes that were Class C legal.

When Arthur Davidson, the last surviving founder, died in a car accident in late December 1950, the engineering department had already begun development on a new series of flathead Forty-five engines and bikes designated the K series. A race version, the KR, was planned from the start, to replace the aging WRs. The K models made their debut for the 1952 season.

Equipment and ideas appeared that were adopted from popular English motorcycles. A swingarm rear suspension with shock absorbers improved handling while a foot-operated four-speed transmission with hand clutch got the power more effectively to the rear tire. But the street-going K models and the racing KRs were still Harley-Davidsons, even though they had several forward-thinking features such as the oil-immersed clutch and unit-type construction that placed the engine and gearbox in a common case.

Once again, the first bikes suffered public teething pains. While boasting 56 horsepower, the KRs seemed weaker than the earlier WRs. The telescoping front fork and swingarm rear suspension—improvements on paper—made the bikes handle worse on the track.

The new-style clutches failed. And of course, the engine leaked oil. The shared case for the gears and engine required dismantling even for simple adjustments. Once again, the company stuck with it, working at the same pace as it had gone before to solve development problems. It took less than a season to sort it out and get it right.

In Peoria in the summer of 1952, at a Tourist Trophy event, weather played a role as rain had washed away the topsoil. The advantage and the checkered flag went to Harley's torquey rut-diggers. Bill Miller won Harley's first major event on a KRTT.

In 1953, Joe Leonard won four national events and the Peoria TT, and Paul Goldsmith won Daytona. Out of 18 national events in 1954, KR riders won 13, giving Harley rider Joe Goldsmith the championship and the right to wear the Number 1 plate for 1955. Brad Andres won five nationals outright in 1955, always on KRs and took the plate from Goldsmith. More than a few journalists and countless fans began speaking of Harley's New Wrecking Crew.

It had taken an open-door and open-minded policy from the factory to make it happen. The goal of Class C was to encourage privateers to return to racing in a class that would be competitive for entrants and exciting for spectators. But it took the inventiveness of outside tuners, the race bike preparers for independent racers, to solve many of the KR's problems. Tom Sifton, a Harley dealer since 1933 and an innate mechanical genius, was so successful that the factory threatened to cancel his dealership franchise unless he revealed to the engineering department his secrets for improving flathead breathing, high-rpm lubrication, adopting magnetos for improving spark, and shaping up chassis engineering and high-speed handling. He refused and a decades-long standoff ensued. The factory liked having its bikes in the winner's circles—as Sifton's riders Joe Petrali and Paul Goldsmith and later, Sam Arena—but it also wanted to be there itself. In the end, Sifton won, both on the track and in Milwaukee. The factory valued his accomplishments too highly to cancel his dealership. Eventually, when he sold his dealership to by-then retired racer Sam Arena, he turned over his secrets to the engineering department.

Sure enough. The AMA's Class C rules had leveled the starting line. Tom Sifton and his colleagues just made certain that everything leaned in Harley's direction when it came to the finish line.

Right: There was no rear suspension on early dirt track KRs. The dirt on top of these ovals cushioned the ride as much as any of the tough young racers needed in those days. Wheelbase was 56 inches, just right for tossing the back end out in the turns to slow the pace from 110 miles per hour or so to about 90.

Chapter 10
Beating Back the English Bullies

It was 1956.

Charlton Heston had come down from the mountain with Ten Commandments. Elvis Presley sang about hound dogs and blue-suede shoes. An oral vaccine was developed for polio. Dwight Eisenhower was reelected President, and Fidel Castro overthrew Cuban dictator Fulgencio Batista. And Superman was leaping tall buildings in a single bound. There was confidence and prosperity in the United States. The birth rate was booming.

Four years earlier, things hadn't been quite so promising. American fighting men and medical crews were still living hor-rific daily experiences in a small, far away Asian country. It would be 20 years before Americans could laugh and cry at a color television show about the exploits of a mo-bile army hospital near the 38th Parallel at the battlefront in Korea.

In 1952, as the Korean "war" raged on, Harley-Davidson introduced its Model K. It wasn't long before motorcycle magazine writers and savvy riders knew it to be a 97-pound weakling. It was equipped with a mild-mannered version of the racing KR engine and gearbox. And it took advantage of the telescoping forks and swingarm rear suspension. But its Forty-five engine wasn't enough. Historian Harry Sucher remembered hunkering down into a racer's tuck on one to see 81 miles per hour. Quickly, the factory offered an optional cams-and-valves kit in a bike known as the KK. But that was only an interim step. And so few were produced that it was actually legendary in its own time. What was still required was a kind of Charles Atlas body-building course. The engine needed strength. Bulking up wouldn't hurt either. So in 1955, the Engineering Department introduced an enlarged version with bigger valves that displaced 55 cubic inches, 883cc. Instead of 30 horsepower, it had about 38 with no weight gain. Flywheels were changed, as was the clutch and the transmission. Like a great weight-training program, Harley turned fat into muscle,

Above: The XL engine incorporated overhead valves that were housed in new iron heads. Their shape resembled an overturned spoon or shovel. Sometime after 1966, when the new Big Twin engine was introduced with similarly shaped heads, the name "Shovelhead" was coined. But Sportsters were called "Ironheads"; the Shovelhead nickname was reserved only for the Big-Twins. Reflected in the optional chrome air cleaner are the shining cylinder heads and the yellow fuel tank of the KHK.

Opposite: In the foreground, the 1956 KHK shows off the last of the 55 ci flatheads, discontinued with this model. The 1957 XL in the background shows off everything else it carried over from its predecessors. The engine was the only dramatic change.

Above: The predecessor to these 1956 KHK's was the Model K, introduced in 1952 to replace the long-lived and by then, long-in-the-tooth Model WL. The Model K brought to Harley riders many innovations all in one $865 package. Rear suspension (a swingarm controlled by diagonal shocks on each side) and unit construction (crankcase and gearbox in one housing) were two of the most obvious improvements.

Left: Another significant innovation introduced with the Model K and carried over onto the Models KH and KHK was foot shift and hand clutch. Options—always a part of Harley's catalog—for the KH and KHK included the Deluxe Group for the KH models, which featured 18 different chromed pieces, as shown here. It cost an extra $94 in 1956.

Opposite: The first K engine had a 2.75x3.81-inch bore and stroke, for a 45 ci displacement from the 45-degree twin. The striking heads were removable flatheads; side valves were part of the cylinder housing. In 1954, stroke was lengthened to 4.56 inches, increasing overall displacement to nearly 55 cubic inches (883cc) for the new Model KH. For 1955 and 1956, a high-performance version of the KH was offered: the KHK, which featured near-racing cams and a highly polished head.

Above: There are more than a few physical similarities between the last high-performance Model KHKs and the new-for-1957 Sportster. It earned its "X" designation by following the U, V, and W flathead twin engines. While the KHK had sold only 1,163 in its two years of life, the new Sportster sold 1,983 in its first year, at a retail price of $1,103.

Right: When Harley-Davidson introduced the new Sportster XL in late 1956 for the 1957 model year, the sound heard around America was the sad sigh of young riders who had scraped and scrimped to buy a new KHK just months earlier. Showroom windows across America must have been smeared with sweaty palm prints.

keeping the weight the same yet increasing power. The KH would do 95 miles per hour and at more sedate speeds, return 41 miles to every gallon of gasoline.

And still the English bullies with their OHV big singles and twins kicked sand. A KL model was being developed in the back rooms in Milwaukee. It was a significant change, opening the V-angle to 60 degrees. But considerations of space within the frame, and time and money to complete the development forced the project to be shelved before it was accomplished. In the end, the company introduced an ultimate level of optional bits and pieces for the KH. Called the KHK, it was essentially a KR for the street. It pieced together the best of the KK and KH. Parts came from the racing department and were fitted on the production line. Those parts were impossible to recognize from the outside of the bike but riders knew immediately. However, it could also be fitted with other parts, things from the accessory catalog.

Above: The new Sportster engine displaced 55 cubic inches (883cc), just like the KHK's. However, it was reconfigured with a 3.00-inch bore and 3.81-inch stroke. The swingarm rear end with its two shocks was a straight carryover from the Ks.

Left: Foot-operated gear shift was carried over from the Model KH, and it stayed on the left side. (Left-side shifters would not be required by federal standards until 1975.) Chrome trim, Jubilee horn, and other features and gadgets were part of the Deluxe Group option carried over from the Model K bikes.

Bottom: Wheelbase was 57 inches, horsepower was 40, fuel capacity was 4.4 gallons with reserve, tires were 3.50x18 inches, the color was Pepper Red with black tank panels and red fenders, the front forks were hydraulic, the case cover said Sportster, and the bike was a runaway success.

Customers with a KHK could buy a windshield, extra lights, chrome trim, touring handlebars, a second seat, and saddlebags to turn a racer into a fully dressed tourer, though it's doubtful anyone ever did. In any event, it still wasn't Charles Atlas, but that was because the factory knew something it wasn't ready to tell. The KHK was short-lived, and the KL was stillborn because Harley-Davidson had a new set of letters coming. Charles Atlas was getting new initials: XL and OHV.

The XL, or the Sportster as it was cast in relief on its transmission cover, arrived in 1957 with new heads with overhead valves. The powerplant internals were shifted around to retain the 883cc displacement while creating a short-stroke engine. This allowed larger valves to work in the head, and the shorter stroke allowed the engine to turn faster. This was the combination for power the English bullies had been using for years.

In fact, the whole thing got quite complicated. Flatheads had valves coming up alongside the cylinders, operated by valve-lifters. The Sportster's overhead valves operated off the same four cams from the valves operated off the same four cams from the KH engine, but the overhead valves required pushrods. These were now routed through the old lifter blocks, up into the heads to rocker arms that pushed the valves down to open them. New cast-iron heads got a new valve cover that was a flatter knuckle, something more like an overturned spoon. Or a shovel.

The compression ratio of this new ironhead Sportster engine was 7.5:1 and that, with all the other improvements, was good for 40 horsepower at 5,500 rpm. A year later, for 1958,

Above: The Deluxe Group for the 1957 XL included chrome handlebars, stainless handlebar clamp cover, chrome headlight, polished instrument panel cover, chrome gas cap and oil tank cap, polished steering damper knob, and many other pieces. Omitting the front safety guard, the Deluxe Group cost only $81.50.

Bottom: The KH sold for $935 in 1956, and the KHK Special Speed Kit was a $68 option, factory installed. Champion Yellow with black tank panels was a standard color. One optional color combination was offered, Flamboyant Metallic Green with white panels and matching green fenders; its cost for the flamboyant owner was an additional $5.

The second-generation Sportster XLCH was conceived as a California-only motorcycle, delivered to dealers as a club sport bike—a scrambler without lights, mufflers, or battery. The rear fender would be "bobbed," shortened to resemble the dirt oval racers. The "C" apparently stood for California, but there were a variety of entertaining rumors suggesting that the "H" meant "hot." Or did the "C" mean "competition" and the "H" mean "highway"? Officially, of course, the XL was the baseline Sportster, and the "H" that had designated "heavy duty" until 1951 changed to denote "high compression" after that.

Harley-Davidson introduced the XLH—H again representing higher compression and higher performance. The ratio was increased to 9.0:1, and the heads got even bigger valves. While this was an improvement, the biggest beaches with the most bullies were in California.

California dealers had influenced the company for years. Fred Ham's record run around Muroc Lake was sponsored by Harley's dealer in Pasadena. Tom Sifton had shown the racing department that it could be done better, without telling them how. The dealers joined forces and asked the factory for a stripped Sportster. (The Sportster was not Harley-Davidson's first named motorcycle, but Sportster buyers had to have grandfathers riding in the nineteen-teens to remember the Silent Gray Fellows.) This new version was intended as a club sport bike.

The factory considered the possibility and agreed, provided the California dealers would guarantee orders of 60 bikes. It would be delivered without front fender or headlight and with a shortened—or bobbed—rear fender. It would use magneto ignition, have straight pipes, no battery and the small (1.9 instead of 4.4 gallon) gas tank. The lights, fenders, mufflers, and a small battery were available as a $60 option, dealer installed. The factory coded it the XLCH.

The myth says that this all stands for "California Highway" or "Competition Hot." Logic suggests it was staid, conservative, Midwest Harley-Davidson simply designating a California version of the XLH for its parts-counter guys who'd have to find spares for it in years to come. Delivered as a dirt-bike scrambler, it often appeared optioned, racing up and down Pacific Coast Highway and Sunset Boulevard. As a clubman special, it sold almost four times the California dealer's 60-bike requirement, 239 in 1958. And everywhere it won. Trophies at drag races, pink slips at stoplights, and hearts and dates at the diners.

The standard weighed 505 pounds and would run the quarter-mile in 15.5 seconds, at 84 miles per hour. The 0-to-60-mile-per-hour times were 7.4 seconds. The California Sportster, weighing 480 pounds, got down the quarter-mile in 14.3 seconds at 92 miles per hour. It hit 60 miles per hour in 6.2 seconds, and it was probably good for 115 miles per hour. The factory published a top speed of 122 miles per hour but that calculated to reaching redline in fourth gear, a theoretical speed, not one observed. But this was America.

Despite the Dwight Eisenhower–approved interstate highway system that was ribboning the country with wide, smooth, divided four-lane raceways, the United States had speed limits unlike the open autobahns and autoroutes of Europe. Top speed only meant how many nights the rider spent in jail. Whether it was at the start line of the local drag strip or at the intersection of the state highway, it was the stoplight that mattered in America.

Above: The XLCH—and all Harley-Davidsons in 1958—were offered in four standard colors, this one known as Skyline Blue. The tank sides were Birch White. The factory would only produce this motorcycle if California dealers would take a minimum of 60. The Milwaukee maker underestimated its appeal; 239 sold in 1958 and another 1,059 in 1959.

Opposite: The engine dimensions remained unchanged. Bore and stroke were still 3.00x3.81 inches with total displacement of 55 cubic inches. It was possible to squeeze as many as 60 miles per gallon out of the XLCH but it was most often involved in competition—either organized or impromptu—and so fuel economy suffered from the spirited throttle twisting.

Above: Full fenders, mufflers, lights, were all part of a $60 option that was only dealer installed. The Deluxe Group filled out all the chrome possibilities as well. Another option, the SP#3, was called the "higher road-clearance kit" for standard XL and XLH models. This was a purely "scrambler" preparation, equipped with Goodyear Grasshopper tires meant for canyon or desert running off the road.

Left: Wheelbase for the XLCH was the same as for the standard XL, 57 inches, while the XLCH's engine output was more than 50 horsepower, compared to the XL's 40 horsepower. The XLCH remained in production for more than two decades, selling thousands through 1977. It opened Harley-Davidson's eyes to the possibilities of catering to the performance street rider.

Chapter 11
The Myth Meets Hollywood

In a 1930 Howard Hughes film, brothers Monte and Roy Rutledge, played by Ben Lyon and James Hall, were students at England's Oxford University. At the beginning of World War I, they both volunteered for the Royal Flight Corps. Roy became a pilot, Monte a machine gunner and bombardier. The first half of the film got them through flight training, and it established Roy as the level-headed responsible brother and Monte as the emotional philosopher.

Early in the second hour, Roy, now a lieutenant, went into a small French village near where they were based to visit his girlfriend, recent–Howard Hughes discovery Jean Harlow. He rode in on a Harley-Davidson Model J fitted with a sidecar. Arriving in the village in fine spirits, he splashed mud on a couple of officers and was later chastised by a third one for "having it rather soft, being able to dash about the countryside."

The next night, things got tougher. The two volunteered for what was certainly a suicide mission, flying a captured German Gotha bomber back to Germany to use it to destroy a munitions depot that had cost English fliers and infantry many lives. After receiving their preliminary orders, the two were free until flight time. Back in their quarters, they made plans for the evening.

"Do you think they'll let us have a motorcycle?" Monte asked Roy.

"Why, of course," Roy answered, smiling pridefully, "we're *it* tonight."

Monte turned away from his saving mirror to look at Roy.

"We're it, alright," he said.

The brothers got their Harley-Davidson and went into town one last time, Roy planning to spend the evening with Harlow. But she had gone out with another officer and so Roy and Monte got drunk. Following some soul-searching, the two

Above: The story goes that two versions of this bike were built for the 1969 movie *Easy Rider*. In typical motion picture production procedure, one was used for longer traveling shots and another, generally referred to as a "hero" was used for close-ups. Shortly after the end of filming, the hero was stolen from its storage area. And of course the second bike was crashed in the film's final scenes.

Opposite: *Captain America* sported one of the most famous gas tank paint jobs ever. The 13-stripe, 25-star logo came to signify everything American youth stood for and everything it rebelled against. The Panhead twin put out about 55 horsepower at 4,800 rpm.

returned to the airfield and took off in the bomber, emblazoned with a mascot and took off in the bomber, emblazoned with a mascot painted on its rear fuselage. It was a skull with an arrow descending through it. The film was titled *Hell's Angels*.

In it, the motorcycle was transportation, the way to get around the countryside for dashing pilots in the RFC. It was a prop, historically correct, and it also went further to establish more of the character of the two brothers.

In 1933, Groucho and Harpo Marx in their film *Duck Soup* made use of a Harley Model J and sidecar as transportation. It was "his excellency's car," and Groucho was "his excellency." Repeatedly, either the motorcycle or the sidecar—wherever Groucho was not—took off without the other attached.

Four years later in 1937, Larry, Moe, and Curly used a flathead and sidecar in their Three Stooges comedy, *Playing the Ponies*. With Curly riding in the sidecar and Moe driving, the two paced a racehorse to win. At the finish line, Moe stopped and Curly didn't, flying out of the car and face first into the dirt.

Other than U.S. Army Motorcycle Corps training films, the next major appearances by motorcycles in Hollywood productions waited until well after World War II had ended. Of course, a new war had begun, triggered by the *Life* magazine cover and an exaggerated report of the incident at Hollister. The motorcycle in these new films represented much more than just a dashing or comical transportation prop.

In Stanley Kramer's *The Wild One* in 1953, Marlon Brando played an introspective young man named Johnny Strabler. Johnny led the BRMC (Black Rebels Motorcycle Club), an "outlaw" gang. Outlaw clubs had begun to appear after the war, groups at odds with the American Motorcycle Association's (AMA) standards of regulated competition and behavior. (At the time, the AMA was so legitimate that events within California were sponsored by the California Highway Patrol.)

The film opened with a long view down a country road. The soundtrack was filled with a crying saxophone. Kramer assaulted viewers with these words on the screen: "This is a shocking story. It could never take place in most American towns—but it did in this one."

"It is a public challenge not to let it happen again."

In the opening scenes, a Highway Patrol officer who has run off Brando's group, talked with a race official as the gang rumbled away.

"Where did that bunch come from?" the officer asked.

"I don't know," the official shrugged. "Everywhere. I don't even think they know where they're goin'. Nutty. Ten guys like that gives people the idea everybody that drives a motorcycle is crazy. What are they tryin' to prove?"

Opposite: In 1969, a couple of motorcycles were designed for film fame. They had started their lives as stock, 74 ci, OHV foot shift motorcycles. But when producer Peter Fonda—soon to be known as Wyatt in his film *Easy Rider*—went looking for reasonably priced used motorcycles to convert into Captain America's custom chrome ride, he and executive producer Bert Schneider found pay dirt at the police auctions. Fonda's mechanics kept the engines and discarded the rest.

Below: The Panhead OHV engine had been introduced in 1948 as the update the venerable Knucklehead Big Twin. Bore and stroke were 3.43x3.96 inches. The pans at the top of the heads replaced the Knucklehead's stamped-steel rocker-arm covers in another attempt to stop oil flow onto riders' legs.

"Beat's me," the officer replied. "Lookin' for somebody to push them around so they can get sore and show how tough they are .…."

Mary Murphy and Lee Marvin joined Brando in the three lead roles. Murphy played Kathy Bleeker, daughter of the town's policeman and a waitress for her uncle at Bleeker's Café and Bar. Marvin played Chino, the leader of a wilder gang.

When Johnny's gang took over Bleeker's bar—albeit politely: they paid for drinks and danced with local girls—one of the girl's learned the meaning of the club initials.

"Black Rebels Motorcycle Club." She repeated. "That's cute. Hey Johnny! What're you rebelling against?"

Brando, tapping his hands in drum beats to the jazz on the jukebox, deadpanned. "What've you got?"

And everybody, riders, and locals alike, laughed. Most of Brando's behavior throughout the film alternated between being basically a nice guy and fighting that instinct down so he could be a silent, forceful tough guy. But even in his toughest moments when his actions spoke for him, it was clear it was an act that caused him inner turmoil.

Lee Marvin stole the show as the grubby, reckless, antisocial comedian. His jokes were aimed at whatever community he stopped in. Marvin's character wore a cloth aviator's helmet with goggles and a four-day growth of beard and rode a Harley flathead missing a few parts. Brando wore a clean motorcyclist's cap—something similar to a police uniform cap—that was always at a jaunty angle even while riding his Triumph.

Of course, in 1953, this was terrifying. Hollister was gone but not forgotten. Kramer, an experienced producer, recognized the value of a good, familiar story, well told. Despite on-screen credit to Frank Rooney for the story, this tale had numerous similarities to the facts and fictions of Hollister. By turning the film into a modern-day cowboy movie—new gun rides into town, sees girl, gets girl, has big fight, rides away from girl and town—audiences knew what to expect. The fact that Kramer put the cowboys on motorcycles merely updated the genre.

Just before the climax of the film, Murphy and Brando had ridden off into the night. He had helped her escape a kind of Indians-circling-the-wagons attack. Murphy then challenged Brando, asking him why he hated everybody. He didn't answer and Murphy, hoping to keep the conversation going, looked at the motorcycle and softened.

"I've never ridden on a motorcycle before," she said, leaning against the front fork. "It's fast. It scared me. But I forgot everything. It felt good. Is that what you do?"

Fifteen minutes later when the film ended, Brando still hadn't answered her question. But he didn't need to. And it wouldn't have mattered to her or anyone whether he rode out of town on a Triumph or a Harley or a pale horse.

Hollywood waited a few years again before venturing into motorcycling. Its next attempt seemed to exist only to provide

The bike was substantially modified, its frame laid back slightly, its head raked outward, and its front forks lengthened by 12 inches. The stock FL police frame and components were scrapped, replaced by a rigid wishbone frame along with many custom parts.

plenty of screen time to motorcycle chrome and gratuitous violence. It went on that way until the late 1960s when novelist Terry Southern and friends Peter Fonda and Dennis Hopper revisited the story of Don Quixote and his faithful sidekick Sancho Panza, an idealistic knight and his aide gone off in search of adventure.

In a moment of visual irony barely 15 minutes into their 1969 film *Easy Rider*, Wyatt, known throughout the film as "Captain America" (played by Fonda), and Billy (played by Hopper) wheeled Fonda's bike into a small desert ranch to change a flat rear tire. Twenty feet away, while Hopper and Fonda removed the rear tire, two ranchers were shoeing one of their horses. The ranchers let down the horse's hoof as the riders set the bike back onto the ground. A moment later, when

invited to share the rancher's family meal, Fonda complimented the man on his home, land, and life.

"It's not every man," Fonda observed, looking around admiringly, "who can do his own thing in his own time." And with that, Don Quixote and Sancho Panza—make that Fonda and Hopper—rode off in search of adventure.

Fonda rode a heavily customized, intensely chromed Panhead. Its tank—and his occasionally worn helmet—were painted in stars and stripes. Tall and extremely lean, he was dressed in black leather from neck to foot with the American flag sewn into his jacket back. Hopper was all earth tones and fringe, his Australian bush-style hat strapped on his head, its brim curled up on the left side. His bike, a less radical Panhead, was painted in red and orange and yellow and hot rod flames.

George Hansen—Jack Nicholson—came into their lives as a drunken, small-town lawyer. His modus operandi was to toast great dead poets with his pint bottle and to buy his way out of any problem. Fonda offered him a ride with a single, fateful question.

"George, you got a helmet?"

Nicholson made a face filled with memory and mirth and confirmed that he did, indeed, have a helmet.

Cut to: Daytime. Exterior. The open road.

Nicholson wore his gold and blue college football helmet, and rode off into the morning light seated behind Captain America.

A day later, the three of them stopped conversation when they entered a Southern small-town café for supper. And then it started again. A group of young girls divided up the motorcyclists among themselves without ever leaving their booth. Nicholson allowed that he'd like to order kidneys because he left his out there on the road somewhere. Instead they got a steady barrage of snide criticism from the locals, and they left without a meal.

Camping later that night, Nicholson lamented what had happened to the country. He tried to explain it all to Hopper, telling Hopper the locals were not afraid of him but they were afraid of what he and Fonda represented to them.

"Hey, man," Hopper laughed, "all we represent to them, man, is somebody who needs a haircut."

"No," Nicholson smiled like a bad card player with a good hand. "What you represent to them is freedom."

Hopper asked him what was wrong with that. Nicholson agreed there was nothing.

"But talking about it and being it are two different things. It's real hard to be free when you are bought and sold in the marketplace," Nicholson continued. "But don't ever tell anybody they aren't free because they're gonna get real busy killin' and maimin' to prove to you that they are … Oh yeah, they're gonna talk to you and talk to you and talk to you about individual freedom. But they see a free individual, it's gonna scare 'em.

"It makes 'em dangerous," Nicholson said.

And in the camp in the swamp in the night, the dangerous locals paid a visit to the free men. With ax handles, they beat Fonda and Hopper. And they killed the lawyer.

A sign in the library of a New Orleans bordello caught Fonda's eye. "Death only closes a man's reputation," it read, "and it determines it as good or bad." After their short visit to the Mardi Gras, Hopper and Fonda, held back by the lowered seats on their lengthened bikes and pulled forward by their distant handlebars, headed out, riding on to meet a green pickup truck on a lonely road to pay the price for their freedom.

In the early 1970s, Michael Parks starred in a television series about a young newspaper journalist named Jim Bronson. In the 1969 pilot, he ended up with a Sportster and no job, so he set off to travel across America, to find work and experiences as they came to him.

Each episode began with a scene that became inspiration for thousands of youngsters and couch potatoes as Bronson, his black stocking cap on his head, rode up alongside a felt-hat and black trench coat–clad family-man caged in his huge station wagon at a stoplight.

Bronson's Sportster bore no Harley-Davidson logos, but on the red peanut tank, the symbol of the pyramid with the eye from the back of a one-dollar bill, stared out. A small bag was strapped over the headlight, and a helmet and a larger duffel was tied against the small sissy bar behind him.

Interrupted from his reverie of worry over paying bills and placating his boss, the station wagon driver would look over and speak to Bronson.

"Taking a trip?"

"Yeah."

"Where to?"

"Oh, I dunno. Wherever I end up, I guess."

The man inside the station wagon would rub his face. And then he would speak again.

"Boy I wish I was you."

Bronson would smile almost sheepishly.

"Well, hang in there."

Every week, Jim Bronson, a good guy dressed mostly in black, eyes hidden behind his Ray-Bans, would ride away from this guy and head for another opportunity to simply help people.

Then Came Bronson appeared on the small screen at a time when most movie theaters were showing films that portrayed the opposite impression of riders and their motorcycles. Films like *Born Losers* (1967), *Hells Angels On Wheels* (1967), *Angels from Hell* (1968*), Naked Under Leather* (1968), *The Glory Stompers* (1968), *The Angry Breed* (1969), *Cycle Savages* (1969), *Angel Unchained* (1970), *Black Angels* (1970), *Chrome and Hot Leather* (1971), and dozens of others from the same period rehashed the warning to all civilized citizens that associating with motorcyclists could be hazardous to their health.

In the style of the late 1960s, upholstery was tucked and rolled on the narrow buddy saddle. It became the perch for *Easy Rider* co-star Jack Nicholson. The hardtail ride prompted Nicholson to joke in a restaurant that he'd order the kidneys because he'd left his somewhere on the road behind them.

It wasn't until a 1985 film by Peter Bogdanovich that motorcycle gang members began to look less menacing. Based on a true story, *Mask*, starred Cher as Florence (Rusty) Dennis, a young woman in Los Angeles' San Gabriel Valley who had a seriously diseased son.

Rusty was a cynical and seasoned woman. Her best friends were a group of bikers known as the Turks who partied hearty. Her son Roy, called "Rocky" and played in the film by Eric Stoltz, dreamed and plotted his way on the map to take a Harley-Davidson ride across Europe. As his disease worsened, Rusty would hold her teenage son and encourage him to tell her stories about his future trip to Europe, to get his mind off the pain. He told her his dreams of a '74 Shovelhead with a suicide shift. He dreamed it was painted bright red.

Mask is probably one of the few movies ever to portray black-leather clad motorcycle riders as people like everyone's neighbors. In the film they were compassionate characters who earned and deserved viewer sympathy. Both Cher and Stoltz received critical acclaim for their portrayals of mother and son. It was a story about people with hopes and dreams and problems and tragedies who—by coincidence—also rode motorcycles.

In *Easy Rider*, the lost generation that was stretched out and pulled taut by their custom bikes, got paid back by the "squares" for the excesses of Hollister and Stanley Kramer's vision. Bikes were co-stars to the actors and actresses with speaking parts. Only the bikes didn't get equal credits. In both films, art mimicked reality. It would be another half-generation before reality would mimic art. It would take *Mask* to swing perspective back to the middle of the scale.

By 1990 the myth had been examined and explained and, so far as the silver screen was concerned, it had been dissected. What remained was to reassemble it all as "mystique." Walt Disney did exactly that in a 1991 picture directed by Joe Johnson. The film featured Bill Campbell as Cliff Secord, an around-the-pylons airplane racer in Los Angeles in 1938. It co-starred Alan Arkin as his boss, Peevy. Campbell got an unexpected chance to try a new kind of flight when he and Arkin found a one-man rocket. Invented by Howard Hughes for demonstration at the 1939 New York World's Fair, the rocket had been stolen and hidden under the seat of an old plane in a hangar they rented.

Clifford arrived at the airfield on race day—as he arrived anywhere, any day—on his Harley-Davidson JDH. Within minutes he was off into the air to save the day with the rocket strapped to his back. His motorcycle was part of the character and costume of the man known as The Rocketeer. This latest film version was a continuation of the line begun in 1903 when Bill Harley and Walter Davidson redefined basic transportation. As basic transportation, it was appropriate to this character; the mystique was finally distilled pure, clear.

It would be impossible to imagine that the young airplane racer/rocket flier would arrive for work every day behind the wheel of a Studebaker six-window sedan.

He just had to ride the hottest Harley-Davidson available.

Right: This replica was commissioned by the late Otis Chandler for his Vintage Museum collection. It was built by Glenn Bator after hundreds of hours spent studying publicity still photographs, video tapes of the film, and dozens of conversations with members of the cast and crew. Bator rides here.

Chapter 12
The Last Panheads, the First Button Pushers

In introducing its new engines in 1948, Harley-Davidson once more acknowledged its ongoing problem. Even though the total-loss oiling systems had been replaced by a closed pressurized version that returned oil to its separate tank, the motorcycles were still a partial-loss oil system.

In an attempt to solve the problem once and for all, the engineers designed new cylinders and new heads for both the Sixty-one and Seventy-four Big Twins. Like the old cylinders, these were cast iron. But the heads were now cast from an aluminum alloy to reduce weight and shed heat better. A higher-capacity oil pump was fitted and oil lines and lubrication passages were moved inside the cylinder barrels to try again to get rid of oil outside the engine.

Inside the engine, the oil was put to a new use, lifting the valves. Hollow valve lifters were filled with oil, and the oil pressure maintained the clearance necessary for the engine to inhale and exhale without crashing valves into pistons or making too much valve clatter. This technique of hydraulic valve lifters became common in both the motorcycle and automobile industry very soon after Harley-Davidson adopted it.

But the most noticeable change with this new engine was its valve covers. These new baking-tin-sized covers enclosed not only the rocker arms and valve stems but also the top cooling fins. These large metal covers soon earned the engine the nickname Panhead. The pans were lined with a felt pad glued to the pan. The felt pads absorbed oil and noise.

Panheads stuck with the Knucklehead bottom-end. There had not been any complaints about the previous versions to merit changes, so engineering had concentrated on the continuing problems.

One year into the model, in 1949, telescopic forks were introduced. These allowed greater front wheel travel, softening

Above: Electra-Glide followed the pattern the company began with the Hydra-Glide in 1949. That name designated the hydraulic front forks on both 61 and 74 ci bikes. The 1958 Duo-Glide put shocks on the rear as well. In 1956, electric start was added, and the new Big Twin was named Electra-Glide. The new model was offered in black, Hollywood Red, and the optional Hi-Fi Blue or Hi-Fi Red.

Opposite: The FLFB Super Sport could also be had with the King of the Road Option. This included the Solo windshield (in body-matching color), white fiberglass saddlebags, directional signals, and chrome safety guard. The standard FLH sold for $1,530.

the ride because the tall enclosed towers could accommodate longer, softer springs. These forks were oil-filled, and this technology prompted Harley-Davidson to invent the name Hydra-Glide.

The Hydra-Glide offered tourers a level of ride comfort never before possible. And Harley-Davidson, which had long sold its own accessories, had a catalog full of objects to enhance long rides. Windshields and wide soft seats had been available for years, as had saddlebags, first in leather and then in plastic for 1954 and later. Optional luggage racks, driving lights, rearview mirrors, fender skirts, and reflectors dressed up the big Panheads. Owners began covering every inch of their big bikes with options and pieces so that a new name was born just to describe these machines: "dressers."

At the other end of the scale, riders emotionally and financially distant from the dressers began removing pieces, to lighten up both the weight and look of their bikes. In fact, fenders were literally chopped off the bikes using hacksaws. Shifter linkages were shortened and simplified, removing them from the tank and using only short levers right out of the transmission. Big tanks were exchanged for the tiny "peanut" tanks of other models. Anything that could be removed without affecting performance was removed.

This kind of modification was frowned upon by Harley-Davidson and its dealers. What's more, the customers who sought this kind of work met with distrust and dislike because

of their resemblance to recent film portrayals. The work they wanted done—some riders even removed front brakes in order to save weight; going fast was the main objective, stopping was merely an afterthought—made the bikes potentially dangerous or unsafe. So independent shops that had done tuning and speed modification in the past now took on these new tasks as well. As specialists to this special trade, these outsiders became known as "chopper" shops.

At the end of the 1952 season, Harley-Davidson discontinued production of the Sixty-one and at the same time introduced a significant change, adopted from the Model Ks. The company reversed the shift and clutch, operating the clutch by the left hand and the gear shift by the left foot. The hand-operated clutch got help from a strong spring to manage the pressure that had been provided by stronger leg muscles. Hand shift

Opposite: This was the bike that separated dressers from choppers. Fully "dressed," the FLH weighed nearly 700 pounds and guaranteed a comfortable ride at highway speeds across the country. For some riders, it represented all that had gone wrong with motorcycles.

Below: For 1965, the Panhead engine now had a 12-volt electric system and started at the push of a button, although the new starter was still supplemented with the kick start. Engine output was up to 60 horsepower, at 5,400 rpm. A total of 4,800 of the FLH-engined Big Twins were sold.

and foot shift were offered in tandem through the end of the Panhead line.

The Panhead era was one marked by continuing change and improvement. The FL engines got new main bearings and cases for the 1955 model year. This improved reliability by increasing the strength of the individual parts. For 1958, a rear suspension with a swingarm and dual shock absorbers was introduced. This version was called the Duo-Glide to signify working suspension at both ends of the bike.

The ongoing upgrading continued behind the scenes in Milwaukee until 1965 when Harley introduced 12-volt electric starting to their Big Twin (the feature had been introduced on the Servi-Car the previous year). It added a considerable weight penalty to the bikes, but the convenience was worth it to many first-time buyers. And Harley-Davidson, happy with its new winner, was not about to change any of the elements that had brought success to the Panheads. Yes, the usual combination of alphabet codes still persisted. The FLHB was born. But a name was clearer, and it had more appeal to the same newcomers attracted to electric start. Harley called it the Eletra-Glide.

By 1965, Harley-Davidson had achieved with absolute certainty the goal the founders set forth 62 years earlier. They wanted to produce reliable transportation. In the years between founding and electric-start, they had attempted and experimented and achieved and accomplished. But the kick starter required the rider to understand all the variables required to make engines combust for the first time. Gas. Air. Spark. Timing. Engine cold? Engine hot? It could vex even an experienced rider.

Author Allan Girdler put it best in his book *Harley-Davidson: The American Motorcycle* when he wrote, "Nothing you can do with boots on is as satisfying as kick-starting a big bike …. Kick starting means you know what you're doing."

But Girdler went on.

"Electric starting means you know the engine will start."

This was a kind of gift. It meant the motorcycle was reliable transportation. It meant the weekend stretched a little longer. Electric starting meant that riders could have an extra cup of coffee in the morning. Then they could still ride the Harley to work and know that they would not be late.

1969 Aermacchi CRTT-350 Road Racer

Opposite: Aermacchi turned out these racing bikes at the rate of about 30 per year. The Italian company had begun life as an aircraft manufacturer but by the time Harley-Davidson purchased it in 1961, they were producing 250cc singles that fit a market Harley wanted to penetrate.

Left: It's racing. Cut away all extraneous material, even metal housings surrounded the flywheel. Because it was protected by fiberglass fairings, it was not quite so exposed as this. The single cylinder was fed by a Dell'Orto carburetor.

Above: Avon racing tires and Borrani rims—just like Ferraris, Maseratis, and Aston Martins—Ceriani Grand Prix front forks, Koni rear shocks, and magnesium drum brakes were part of the specifications of the Tourist Trophy 350cc bikes that raced throughout Europe under the Harley-Davidson banner.

If you lived here, you'd be home now. If you lived somewhere else, you could still get to here on an Electra-Glide. This was the first of the fully convenient cruisers and just one more in a continuous line of comfortable Big Twin getaway motorcycles.

Chapter 13
The AMF Rescue

By 1969 Harley-Davidson had gone public, offering and selling more than 1.3 million shares of its stock. The company held a steady 12 to 15 percent of the motorcycle sales in the United States. Although it was before the era of hostile takeovers, mergers were widespread. Those who were interested were polite in their inquiries. Harley's refusals were just as polite.

Except that underneath the surface, the company was on a foundation of shifting sands. European bikes—most especially British twins—had eaten into Harley's once supreme position. The Japanese quick-studies had done their homework well, filling in the niches that the rest of the world missed and adopting a marketing program that flat out refuted Hollister, the Hell's Angels, and *The Wild One*.

So, after much soul-searching in the corporate boardrooms and in the homes of stockholders, Harley-Davidson agreed to sell itself—for shares of stock—to AMF, the American Machine & Foundry Corporation, a vast conglomerate that had swerved away from heavy machinery and foundries and moved toward leisure activities and the paraphernalia necessary for enjoying them. AMF offered 1.5 shares of its stock for every share of H-D stock. By the time the deal was inked, Harley's sales had amounted to only 15,475 motorcycles throughout 1968.

What the merger brought to Harley was more up-to-date management and marketing techniques, research and develop-ment funding, engineering expertise across wider manufacturing and production areas, sharper advertising, and more inventive promotional ideas.

Actor Michael Parks, already a Harley-Davidson enthusiast, got Sportsters to ride for his television series, *Then Came Bronson*. Robert Blake became the quintessential cop aboard his *Electra-Glide in Blue*. And daredevil rider Even Knievel, willing to defy gravity (if not always physics) in ways hill-climbers

Above: The FX was one of Willie G. – known as "Bill" in those days–Davidson's first attempts at adaptive reuse. The distinctive fiberglass rear fender and seat assembly was molded in one piece and created in the shape of the boat-tail classic cars of the 1930s. It came from the options columns of the Sportster order forms.

Opposite: If this was waiting at the train station when the 6:05 commuter came in, it made the day's work almost worth it. The 1971 FX Super Glide was a real work of early 1970s pop culture, part of the "Mod" scene as one magazine reviewer called it. Willie G. painted it in red, white, and blue. This combination was known as "Sparkling America."

never imagined, flew through the air and landed in a Harley-Davidson endorsement contract.

When the dust settled after the acquisition, some front-office personnel changes were inevitable. But one of the most notable—and influential—gave encouragement to William G. Davidson, a grandson of the founders who was currently working in Harley's design department. Davidson had finished his formal education as a designer from the Pasadena, California, Art Center College of Design, a school known for nurturing and then turning out top designers in many fields. But now with AMF running the company and influencing longer-term thinking, he was allowed to shed his corporate white shirt, necktie, and suit, and go out among the customers to find out where the motorcycle company had gone adrift from its loyal supporters.

He let his hair grow, dressed in jeans and leather, and he went out and saw and listened and learned. *What* he saw and heard and learned convinced him that he was right about a project already on his drawing board. It was a bike meant to be an enthusiast's machine. Willie G., as he was coming to be known, introduced it in late 1970. It was known as the Super Glide, and it was produced on a shoestring from existing parts.

Starting with an FLH frame and rear suspension, he used its engine and transmission but added instead the lighter front forks, larger front wheel, and smaller headlight from the XLCH. In an acknowledgement to the influences of the choppers, Willie G. had designed the whole bike to look assembled, not manufactured. Then, in an inspired stroke, he eliminated the

electric starter and the big battery needed to run it. Weight savings. Just like the chopper shops. The final touch was plucking from the Sportster option sheets a single-piece fiberglass seat and rear fender that faired into a recessed taillight. It resembled the stylish boat-tail automotive designs of the 1930s Packards and Dusenbergs.

In the height of the depths of Vietnam, Willie G. ordered it painted in red, white, and blue. Harley-Davidson, love it or leave it. And the critics and magazine reviewers loved it. It was not Harley's fastest bike, nor its heaviest nor its lightest. It was just its most interesting. AMF had given Willie G. the liberty to try to rekindle enthusiast interest in Harley-Davidson. If they got interested enough they'd buy. But AMF knew any company needed to get the buyer's attention first.

Top: Standard glow-in-the-dark Shovelhead power gave about 60 horsepower at 5,500 rpm out of the 74 ci (1200cc) twin. Bore and stroke remained 3.44x3.97 inches. The 12-volt electrical system powered the headlight, horn, instruments and the taillight. But Willie G. reminded buyers of their history: The Night Train was a kick start.

Bottom: Wheelbase was 62.75 inches, seat height was 29 inches. The 543-pound Night Train was capable of spinning its 3.75x19-inch front tires and 5.10x16-inch rears at up to 119 miles per hour. And in 1971 it sold new for $2,190 at the factory.

Opposite: It was called the "Night Train" the first time in Harley-Davidson's advertising and then in the magazines that reviewed it. It probably referred as much to its near seamless powerband as to its New York Central Twentieth Century Limited streamliner tail.

True Interchangability

It grew out of an idea that no one thought would be finished. But Andy Mendez began putting it together in his shop, Top Dead Center, in Oxnard, California, back in 1993. The reactions from his friends and customers were fairly consistent. They were incredulous. Of course, Harley-Davidson had evolved more than changed. Certainly, basic dimensions had remained remarkably similar for more than four decades. Sure, some of the bolt holes did line up. But to build it?

And then to run it?

Mendez calls it the Shovel PanKnuckle. And not withstanding the fact that the company calls its new Blockhead the Evolution engine, this is a true evolution engine. The front head is pure Knucklehead, the rear one is letter-perfect Panhead. The bottom end is mostly Shovelhead. And it runs.

It took very little fudging and jiggling to make it fit. It did surprise Mendez, who specializes in building and rebuilding old—pre-Evo—engines and bikes. It just came together very quickly and easily.

For some time, restorers and collectors have had trouble finding Knuckle barrels. But Panhead barrels are plentiful. For that reason, there is a good business in modifying Knuckleheads to fit Pan barrels, basically by relocating head bolts. Lifter block bolt holes needed to be relocated too but Mendez found he had, in his shop, a head with modified bolt holes. He also had two cases that had problems, with one half of each that was an orphan. The right side was a 1937 Knucklehead. But inside it, where the generator idler gear should be mounted, a previous owner had cut off the boss. So it would never again run a generator. However, the left case was a Shovelhead alternator case with all the electric start pieces intact.

Mendez dummied the engine up on a stand in his shop—without internal pieces—and just left it there for his customers and friends to see. It became kind of a hobby, and one day in his spare time, he went to fit a manifold. He was amazed to see how close it came to lining up. He left it but kept looking at it, thinking more and more that his engine just might work.

So then he got serious. Because the two cases were different they had to be line bored and decked. Panhead barrels are shorter than Knucklehead barrels. So he fitted a spacer plate under the Knucklehead to bring it up to the height where it would work. The plate also restored stock compression.

At first he ran a stock Knucklehead cam. This was fine for the front of the engine, but it caused much too high a lift for the Panhead back end. The rocker arms hit the Pan. He tried a spacer between the barrel and the head. Finally, he ended up having a new cam made, Knuckle and Pan.

When the engine was together, he found he had hanging in his shop an electric-start, rigid-frame oil tank that he'd owned for 15 years. Down off the rafters and onto the bike. When he figured out that in order to make the engine actually work, he needed an outside-oiler Panhead (1963–1965) —and it needed to be for a rear cylinder—he checked his walls and rafters and found that this was the one and only one he had. The Knucklehead generator was remachined and became a toolbox. In all, it took him about six months of spare time, hours invested between paying jobs he took into his shop.

Then he got it to run. With his choice of kick start or electric.

What does it sound like? It sounds like 40 years of engine history bolted up in one tidy package. It sounds like *all* 40 years. Each and every single one of them, hitting one cylinder at a time, first the taller one in front and then the shorter one in back and then ....

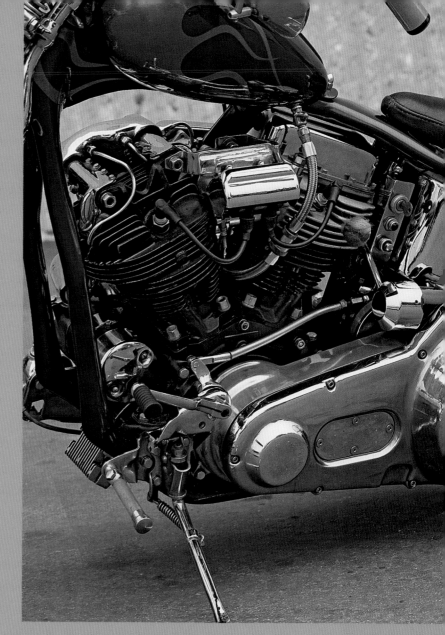

Top: The old generator housing now carries the toolkit. The foot clutch had a return spring to operate like an automobile, known as a "suicide clutch." If the rider lifted his left foot for balance, the bike took off if the hairball shifter was in gear.

Opposite: For years, Harley enthusiasts and engine builders had known that it was theoretically possible to graft together three generations of Big Twin engine components—but to actually do it? Builder Andy Mendez in Oxnard, California, fabricated it to see what would happen. It took nearly six months of spare time to complete in between regular work building and rebuilding pre-Evolution engines for customers. He can start it with a kick or a push of a button. It makes a sweet roar, but one that is definitely confusing to a tuned, experienced ear.

Bottom: The front half of the engine is a Knucklehead cylinder head set on Panhead barrels, and the rear half is a Panhead atop its own barrel. The mixed top end was assembled on a 1971 Shovelhead bottom end. As it came together, builder Andy Mendez was surprised at how well the pieces merged.

Ironically, the buyers cared less for it. Some didn't like the tail. Others, spoiled by electric start, knew another truth as advanced by Allan Girdler: "Looking tough is enough when you know the engine will fire in time for a stylish exit."

After all, the stylish exit was a consideration by this time. Harley-Davidson had movies and television shows. And it had a marvelous product-promoter leaping fountains and stadiums at a single bound. What's more, Harley-Davidson still had Lee Marvin and Peter Fonda.

But great designers know. Sometimes it is necessary to take the customers by the hand and lead them into places they'd never go by themselves. In that way, sooner rather than later, they'll accept the version that was really meant for them. And that will be a great advance over what they bought before or what they could see somewhere else.

The FX sold only 4,700 copies in 1971, compared to 10,000 Sportsters and 6,500 of the other Big Twins. In 1972, the rear fender and seat were changed and 6,500 sold. But

then 10,000 of the FL and FLHs sold along with 17,000 Sportsters. By 1974, when the company gave the FX an "E" and electric start, nearly 6,200 electrics sold compared to about 3,000 purist versions.

There is a quote that investors in fine art use to be philosophical about an unusually high price. They didn't pay too much, they reason. They only paid it too soon.

With the FX, Willie G. didn't do too much. He only did it too soon.

Above: This was the site of Evel Knievel's most famous jump, the attempt to fly over the fountains at Caesars Palace in Las Vegas. He had been negotiating with H-D—an American legend meeting an American icon—but by the time of the jump, the contract was not yet signed. So he flew a Triumph. But he landed on a Harley-Davidson multiple-year endorsement.

Opposite: What's the old line? The worst day on a Harley is better than the best day at work? The FX Super Glide pulled like a freight locomotive running up a long grade. One reviewer ran it from the floor of Death Valley to the highest overlook—285 feet below sea level to 10,000 feet above—and never shifted out of third gear.

Left: Looking down on Knievel's personalized paint work also provides a view of the water-main-sized 36mm Mikuni carburetors. As a racing motorcycle, the earlier series of iron XR-750s with a single carburetor was not very successful. The engines were long on weight and short on power. Still, for Knievel and Harley-Davidson, the arrangement was beneficial. Evel got new, updated bikes before each jump, and AMF-Harley-Davidson got monstrous amounts of publicity.

Above: For Knievel, the problem was never with Harley-Davidson reliability or power. His "races" were always over things—cars, trucks, fountains—so the reliability that escaped the first 200 XR-750s that were built through 1971 had no affect on Knievel. When this bike arrived, however, even the great jumper appreciated the improvements.

Fairly standard road-racing configuration, Knievel's 1972 bike had front and rear brakes. Sometimes these were not needed. The early XR-750s—those built from 1969 through 1971—had a 3-inch bore. The engine was originally a de-stroked Sporster 883cc engine, stroke reduced from 3.81 to 3.22 inches. The second series yielded big changes: Stroke was further reduced to 2.98 inches while bore, in order to maintain a 750cc displacement, was enlarged to 3.125 inches.

Chapter 14
Willie G.'s Voice Becomes Clearer

If the 1971 FX Super Glide was done too soon, it was so that the FXS would arrive on time. This was the Harley-Davidson factory-produced Low Rider, introduced in late 1977. And on time it was, just slightly ahead of people's demand for this kind of bike.

It was really another example of Willie G. taking the pulse of the customers—present and past—and then going shopping in the factory's parts bins before returning to his drawing board. Since the late 1940s, outlaw biker gangs had been modifying their motorcycles to fit their needs and image. These riders had little money, so any changes in their bikes were much more likely to be modification of existing parts. Or their removal. By the late 1960s, many of these outlaws had calmed down, cleaned up, and they had gotten jobs and mortgages and in-laws. The cultural statement that they had spoken by dirty clothes and riding scruffy machines had left them with one strong, sharp memory: riding a motorcycle was immensely satisfying. It cleared their heads, blowing out cobwebs that came in as part of the "square" world's adherence to rules and jobs and family obligations. A motorcycle ride still meant freedom and independence, even if it was only for a few hours. The obligations many of these riders had assumed took from them the free time to do the work on their bikes themselves.

No one really knows where but somewhere in the United States—before Peter Fonda climbed on *Captain America*—someone got the idea of extending the front forks, raking the motorcycle in the same kind of speedboat pose that hot rodders were doing jacking up the front ends of their cars. Bikes got longer, and that became a goal in itself: stretch the motorcycle by increasing the angle of the front forks, by modifying the head lug. (It also became a matter of safety. Raking the stock front

Above: One of the XLCR's most distinctive features was its flat-black, siamesed exhaust pipes. Everything else on the bike was either gloss black or polished aluminum. The twin produced 61 horsepower from cylinders with bore and stroke of 3.19x3.81 inches. Only 1,923 sold in 1977.

Opposite: With 61 horsepower on tap at 6,200 rpm, the rider astride the 530-pound XLCR had 106 miles per hour available right out of the factory. Wheelbase was Sporster-standard 58.5 inches. With forgiving handling, the bike was one of Harley-Davidson's best inventions for mountain roads.

forks brought the center of gravity back down closer to the ground, offering some improvement in balance and handling.)

The early stretched bikes were built on standard frames. Soon customizers like Arlen Ness in San Leandro, California, and others around the country began producing frames specifically for this look. The extended forks were often the solid girder type with additional rails welded on to add length. Front suspensions were minimal, normally just a single spring. And as often as not, front brakes went the way of the chopper's philosophy—stopping is not as important as going.

"Going" on these bikes was somewhat different from riding a factory standard. The shallow steering-head angles of these stretched bikes gave them excellent straight-line stability. But turning was another matter. The additional length required much greater arm strength to pull the front wheel back after a turn. The longer the stretch, the closer the rider came to needing a complete stop just to go around a corner.

The severely stretched front forks were not a long-lived fashion. By the mid-1970s, when motorcycles became objects for show rather than go, it was much more common to see

Above: The XLCR was a curious machine in 1977. Its striking looks were another example of Willie G. Davidson talking to his audience, looking into his crystal ball, and building something slightly ahead of its time. The XLCR was a slow seller. Some dealers just put them away, unsold, an idea in their heads that someday ....

Opposite: In 1977 when the XLCR made its debut, the standard XL-engine was still the 61 ci (1000cc), OHV twin. The red buttons on the cylinder heads cover rockershaft end nuts.

radical rakes and flashy chrome on motorcycles that could be ridden only with great care and concentration into and out of show arenas. Still, a slight rake with slightly extended forks was manageable. It offered the benefit of lowering seating position as well.

So when Willie G. imagined a follow-up to his FX Super Glide, he took another bold leap. He took his FXE and shortened the rear shocks. He gave the front forks a slight rake and even shortened them slightly. Then he scooped out the rider's seat much more deeply than he had done on any previous Super

Harley's Back

The XR-750 appeared hurriedly in time for the 1969 racing season. The AMA, long the nearly blind and almost-deaf uncle to Harley-Davidson racing programs, had finally been pressured into getting glasses and a hearing aid. As a result, it began to let other countries have a more fair chance. So in 1968, the next generation of rules let every 750cc racer in the world compete. Which meant that Harley had its work cut out for it in order to remain competitive.

Racing manager Dick O'Brien's crew began by shortening the stroke of the XL 883cc cast-iron engine that had been the Sportster mainstay. But the engine had problems internally, and the result was a slow, heavy racer. It was beaten by the English and Japanese who'd been recently allowed in to play. By the rules, 200 complete motorcycles were built, a few to be held by the factory. The rest were offered to privateers who weren't interested in buying a loser. Most were scrapped even as the factory was hurrying to produce an alloy engine.

This arrived for the 1972 season, looking nearly identical to the iron failure. But the new engine had heads and cylinder barrels made of more precious metals. Each of the pieces was given larger cooling fins to alleviate the overheating problem the iron engine had under full power load—meaning almost all of a race like the Daytona 200. Two huge Mikuna carburetors stuck out of the new top end. They appeared swept back

So many differences. The early XR-750s had straight silver-painted exhaust pipes on the bike's right side. On dirt tracks, they got dinged and crushed by flying dirt. The new series moved the pipes up high and painted them flat black.

Looks are deceiving. This is not a carryover of the 1969–1971-series of XR-750 factory-built racers. So much was changed during those first three years that it is safe to call this an entirely new machine. By 1972, the legacy of those troublesome original XR-750s was covered in the dirt flung up by the new bikes running away from the crowds of competitors.

into the passing airstream. Inside the engine there was an equally large difference. Bore had been greatly increased and stroke greatly reduced. Output jumped by 10 to 12 horsepower. Ignition was still by magneto, gear driven off the cam gears and mounted below and ahead of the front cylinder. In its first running test in June 1971, it produced 69 horsepower at 6,800 rpm.

Frames came from a Harley-Davidson racing dealer in St. Louis, Earl Widman. Widman provided 250 of these to O'Brien. The original chassis was based on the KR and its engine size and weight. But the XR engine—especially the cast-iron version—was larger and heavier. The frame required major surgery, nipping here, tucking there, bending and flexing here and there,

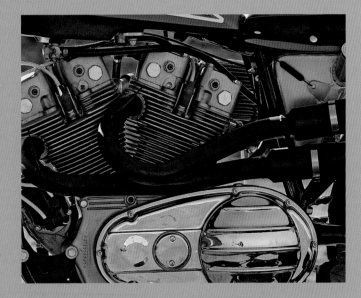

in order to get the bike to handle predictably. When the alloy engine arrived and weighed in 17 pounds lighter than the cast-iron version, things changed again. Ironically, this occurred at just about the same time that manufacturers had learned ways around the rules in order to have separate "production-based" bikes for road racing and for dirt races for both half-mile and one-mile ovals.

Then it was right, all of it, all the time. Harley-Davidson trounced the Triumphs, besotted the BSAs, and nailed the Nortons in race after race. It sent Yamaha and then Honda back home and back to their drawing boards.

But if imitation is the sincerest form of flattery, Harley-Davidson soon learned that Honda was the most sincere. The XR-750 was available to anyone with the cash—in fact, something like 600 have been sold. So Honda bought one, took it home, admired it, dismantled it, copied it, assembled their own—adding by the way, overhead camshafts and four valves per cylinder—and then returned with it to the United States. Then Honda rubbed Harley's face in Milwaukee's own magic.

Top: The big difference is aluminum. Early XR-750s used cast-iron cylinder heads and barrels derived from production Sportster parts. The engines were too heavy and too weak. Beginning in 1972, aluminum alloy replaced the iron and podium finishes began to replace tales of also-rans.

Center: Goodyear tires front and back were factory recommended. Wheel rims were aluminum. The frame was welded tubular steel. Girling racing rear shocks held the rear swingarm in tight control, and front forks were Ceriani; both ends were carried over from the earlier XR-750s. With full tanks, the XR-750 weighed about 320 pounds.

Bottom: The only thing that beat this package was when Japanese invaders bought one from the factory, took it home, and built their own version with four valves per cylinder. Harley's four-stroke engine's broad powerband provided a range of control and subtlety that the volatile two-strokes that Yamaha raced early on against the XR-750 didn't allow. Later Honda and Yamaha tried highly modified versions of their four-stroke street twins, but these bikes only achieved limited success against the XR-750 on the oval tracks.

Opposite: One 36mm Mikuni carburetor blends the mix for each of the 3.125x2.98-inch cylinders. From 45 ci (750cc), horsepower estimates—no tuner would ever give exact figures—are about 90. With mile-track gearing, professional riders have 130-miles-per-hour capability.

Willie G. styled the XLCR with a few racing cues. Its tail was reminiscent of his XR-750 as was the shape of the fuel tank. Its name—CR stood for "Café Racer" – appealed to those whose Sunday rides were sprints from one watering hole to the next.

Glide. This seat was just 27 inches above the ground. He spent money on cast wheels and put on three disk brakes for serious stopping. He used twin fuel tanks in order to get them lower, and he used low, flat handlebars to keep the rider down as well. Customers could have the bike in any color they wanted so long as it was metallic gray, and in another purely styling move, Willie G. specified the engine cases and cylinder barrels and heads done in black wrinkle finish. The he had the fins on the heads polished.

The result was startling, completely unexpected. It was another Willie G. Davidson homage to the less glamorous elements of motorcycling. While magazines were promoting touring and racing, while television and print advertising was trying to clean up motorcycling's image still held over from *The Wild One* and *Easy Rider*, here was a machine that flew right in the face of all of that image-conscious conservatism.

Riders who might not ever have known how to find a chopper shop or locate a custom frame builder looked at—and then bought—the FXS Low Rider. Its seating position allowed shorter riders to graduate from a Sportster to a Big Twin. But it also allowed big riders to dwarf a big machine.

Simply put, it was factory authorized, fully warranted, regular production sex appeal.

When the counting was done at the end of the 1978 model year, the FXS represented almost half of FX sales, and the line outsold everything else Harley produced.

Willie G. Davidson had not stumbled onto something brilliant here. He had taken notes and taken names. The era of the American muscle car was over. The Organization of Petroleum Exporting Countries (OPEC) and a group of insurance companies had seen to that. During that heyday from 1966 through 1972, performance-oriented buyers in the United States could customize a car right out of the factory order books, creating a unique and highly personalized vehicle delivered with a warranty and a factory service organization. But gasoline suddenly sold for 70 cents per gallon. Cars getting eight or nine miles per gallon—and ones

Above: Although there's a dealer tag out back, don't get your hopes up. First-year Low Riders are hard to find, and Harley-Davidson of Glendale, California, owner Oliver Shokouh has no plans to sell this one out of his own collection. In creating the Low Rider, Willie G. shortened the front forks and rear shocks.

Right: Production of the new FXS, the Low Rider, begin in 1977. By year end, 3,742 had been sold. Where Willie G. Davidson had shown some buyers the future with his XLCR Café Racer, he gave others what they wanted right now with the Low Rider.

that cost as much to insure as they had to purchase—made motorcycles look very interesting.

What Willie G. accomplished with the FXS was to take over—single-handedly—what the auto companies had given up when they reacted to gasoline crunches. Ford produced its Mustang II, Chevrolet had its Vega, and Chrysler had its K-cars. The FXS would turn a quarter-mile in 15 seconds, which was about a day and a half sooner than a Vega would get there. The Vega got 26 miles per gallon. The Low Rider would do 47. The Mustang II was available in a luxury trim version designed by the Ghia styling studios in Italy. Polished shoes and clean nails

Harley-Davidson introduced a new frame with the XLCR. It extended the top rails farther back than on models that came before. This allowed the company to move the rear shocks back so that the lower shock mount was directly above the axle on the swingarm. The new shock position improved handling while taking a styling cue from the XR-750.

The Low Rider was powered by the familiar Seventy-four engine that drove the other Harley-Davidson Big Twins. Bore and stroke were 3.43x3.96 inches, providing about 65 horsepower in a big bike weighing 640 pounds, tanks full.

seemed mandatory. By the time Willie G. gave Harley-Davidson customers the Low Rider, they were plenty ready for it. They just didn't know what *it* was until they saw it.

At the same time Willie G. was inventing the FXS he was busy taking notes from another crowd. He already knew the tourers, the riders who dressed out their bikes and rode off across the country self-contained, self-satisfied, and self-sufficient. And comfortable. But the company was already attending to their needs. He had gotten to know the customizers, and he personally was looking after their desires. When he watched the racers, he discovered the wannabees.

This was the crowd that went to the races and then went to their own customizers. They spent money to make their bikes look as much like the racers they admired as they could afford. And then on weekends, they put on their one- or two- piece leather suits, and they rode. Fast. From one spot to the next. From one restaurant to the next gas station and up the hill to

the mountain-top café. Import bikes catered to this café-racer market because import bikes were the ones competing in the real races throughout Europe and in Japan.

The Sportster was a natural platform to use to invade this import stronghold. The XLCH had grown old gracefully, and Willie G. got together with a few wizards in engineering to breathe life back into what was becoming a classic in its own time.

A new frame was created, one that allowed the rear shocks to move to the back end of a squared-box swingarm and that positioned them more vertically (like the racing XR-750). This took care of the on-going flex problem that was always mentioned in contemporary magazine reviews. Wheels were cast alloy, similar to those on the bigger FXS. The engine was standard 1000cc Sportswear fare, but it was given black cases, barrels, and air cleaner, set off by brushed-aluminum rocker covers and chrome-plated pushrod tubes. Exhausts were siamesed, the front and rear joined together right at the base of the V and then split again. Almost everything except the front forks, rear shocks, and the brake rotors was flat black, shiny black, or wrinkle. And it was finished with a small fairing, rear-set foot pegs, and a solo seat, all the better to emphasize its boy-racer influence.

Historians are blessed with perfect vision. But artists and designers—as carefully as they research their market—often shoot in the dark. They're given no information about pesky crosswinds. And no one ever warns them that their target might be moving. Or that there might not even be a target. Many artists and their works are only discovered after they've died. Or when they've quit their art to bag groceries or sell cars or work in a factory.

So Willie G. shot an arrow into the air. It landed square on the bull's-eye. But, like the proverbial tree in the forest, no one was there to hear it or see it hit the blue dot in the center. The XLCR was a bike for no market. It remained in the catalog only through 1978. Slightly more than 3,100 sold in two years. But just like Willie G.'s FX and Low Rider, the Café Racer moved the benchmark much farther long.

Fortunately for Harley-Davidson, AMF had enough money to give Willie G. a quiver of arrows. Because even though some of his brain-children were not sales successes, they were admired by the journalists. Dealers reported traffic in the showrooms— the result of magazine attention to the new machines—even if not everyone had a checkbook in their pocket.

Willie G. boldly took a step backward for 1980. Harley-Davidson introduced his FXB, the model commemorating the rally and races held every August in Sturgis, South Dakota. Leather belts had driven Harley's earliest machines. With the assist of modern technology, belts were back. But the passage of time had given them teeth. Developed with the help of Gates Rubber Company, toothed rubber-and-Aramid-fiber drive belts replaced the primary drive chain inside the primary case and the final drive chain to the rear wheel. Because the belts were wider, some modifications had to be done to the running gear. But the benefits were obvious in terms of reduced noise and maintenance. More than that, they seemed to reduce the engine vibration that was translated to the frame and rider's seat. This was a direct benefit to the rider, a result of AMF's ownership, which had pumped money and blood and sweat and new energy into Harley's engineering department. A young engineer named Erik Buell was deeply involved.

Harley first projected belt life at 20,000 miles, but in actual use, riders got between 30,000 and 40,000 miles. Again, Willie had stretched the two envelopes, one in engineering and technology and the other in customer acceptance. Only 1,470 Sturgis Eighties were produced and not all sold. The best was a radical idea, another arrow shot into the air where there was no target. Riders feared a rubber band slingshot effect on acceleration. They feared slippage and breakage. None of their fears were founded. More than 3,500 belt-drive Sturgis-commemoratives sold in 1981. Buyers liked the ride. Belts began to appear on a wider range of Big Twins.

When Willie G.'s latest arrow landed, it also scored a bull's-eye. Only it hit in a target much larger than anything he'd aimed for before that time.

The office. Low Riders were available only in metallic gray with red lettering in their first year. It was another Davidson styling idea. Distinctive bikes deserved their own colors and only those colors were available during the introductory year.

It's a long drink of water, with its 63.5-inch wheelbase. But what adds to that appearance is the height. Or lack of it. The deeply scalloped seat puts the rider's posterior barely 27.4 inches above the road.

Opposite: This was smart thinking on Davidson's part, getting the factory to build—with a warranty—what the customizers were doing. It wasn't evil corporate America trying to crush the independent. Davidson was a perceptive designer with business sense. Fortunately he worked with absentee owners too occupied with other problems to notice the ripples he caused in motorcycling's pond.

Above: Rubber belt drive greatly improved rider comfort. It was introduced on the 1980 FXB Sturgis following several years of development work with Gates Rubber Company. Ironically, while this toothed belt drive was an engineering advance, it was a stylistic throwback to the first 10 years of the company when leather belts drove the singles and twins.

Above: Initially, engine compression was 8.0:1. While this meant high performance and excellent fuel economy, magazine reviewers found it pinged even on premium fuel. And when lighter riders opted to forgo the electric start in favor of the kick-start, they had to resort to Sportster starting techniques: kneeling on the seat and bringing down their entire weight to bear against the high compression.

Opposite: The company was surprised by the life of its primary drive belt—which stretches from the engine to the clutch—and its main belt, both of toothed rubber. Initially, belt life was expected to be 20,000 miles, but riders found they got double that. The company eventually discontinued the primary belts because engine heat affected them.

Above: This Big-Twin 80 ci (1340cc) Shovelhead engine was introduced in 1980 and produced about 65 horsepower from cylinders with 3.50x4.25-inch bore and stroke. Building on the FXS Low Rider introduced in 1977, Willie G. created the FXB Sturgis by painting everything black. Highway footpegs were factory standard.

Opposite: For one week every year since 1938, Mecca for Harley riders moved west from Milwaukee. It settled each August in the golden hills of northwest South Dakota at Sturgis for the races and rallies. Interrupted for two years by the war, 1980 was considered Sturgis' 40th meeting. For Willie G. Davidson, whose fingers measured the pulse of riders, there was no other name possible for this bike.

Chapter 15
Rapid Transit

In June 1981, a quiet internal revolt freed Harley-Davidson from the benevolent giant that had saved it. Perhaps this was inspired by the Italian businessmen who had purchased Aermacchi back from Harley-Davidson in 1978. They rejuvenated it into a going concern, albeit under a new name, Cagiva, an act that would give faith and courage to any similar group of businessmen/idealists. But wherever the motivation came from, a group of H-D officers and a few outside sympathizers bought the company back from AMF.

AMF had saved the company from the economy, customer attitudes of the times and even from itself. But a decade after buying H-D, AMF began looking more at returning to its core businesses, the manufacture of heavy machinery. It publicly stated its goal was to increase from one-third to at least one-half the proportion of its time, energy, and resources devoted to that work. Handwriting had not yet been scrawled on the walls but the whispers were becoming audible.

One of AMF's significant contributions to Harley-Davidson was its strengthening of the research and development sections of the company and its encouragement of the engineering department. It doesn't matter, in retrospect, whether AMF took advantage of anything that research and development and engineering had created. The foundations and the ideas were there, and they stayed with Harley when AMF departed.

When Harley-Davidson was once again independent, it took advantage. It quickly replaced the Sportster frame with one that was stiffer and lighter. The oil tank was relocated to a position similar to the XR-750 for better balance. Engine compression was decreased to better accommodate poorer quality gasolines available nationwide. The regular production bikes were, overall, generally improved over those that had come before. But none

Above: Based on the lower end of the XL-1000, Harley engineers fitted iron barrels and adapted versions of the aluminum alloy XR-750 racing heads. Twin 36mm Dell'Orto carburetors fed the twin 3.18x3.81 bore and stroke cylinders. Horsepower was quoted as 70.6 at 5,600 rpm (compared to 56 horsepower for the standard XL). Factory-available kits could boost the XR-1000 engine to 90 horsepower.

Opposite: In its own domain, the XR-1000 was Harley-Davidson's meanest street fighter. It was conceived as a street version of the XR-750 race bike, although there was only limited similarity between the two machines. Most XR-750s raced around ovals while most XR-1000s raced under streetlights from one stoplight to the next.

Waiting to go trolling for suckers once the sun has set, the XR-1000 sits at the front door of its business office, the start line of an impromptu street quarter-mile in suburban Los Angeles. But this business required serious capitalization: a new XR-1000 sold for $6,495 at a time when the basic XLX-61 Sportster sold for $3,995.

of the magazine reviewers was yet yelling at their publishers to stop the presses.

So the company stretched a little more. For 1983, they introduced two new Sportsters. One they called the XLX-61. This was a lean, spare machine, meant to fight the Japanese imports for the customer's dollar. Like the Café Racer, it was fitted with a solo seat, but it used the "peanut fuel tank, low handlebars, staggered exhaust pipes, and lowest price—$3,995—anyone had seen on a Sportster in years."

The other machine was much more interesting. It was produced in response to racing fans' requests for a road-going XR-750. The company was hesitant to build it but in the end, cooler heads lost out in one of those rare victories for enthusiasts, and the XR-1000 was shipped to eager dealers. The XR-1000 was given aluminum pistons from the XR-750 and mated to the

racer's alloy heads. These were connected in the middle with new cast-iron cylinder barrels. Dual Dell'Orto carburetors swung off toward the rear just like the racing bike's Mikunis. It took a great deal of nudging and coaxing to get the engine assembled and to fit it into the frame. The completed bike yielded several results. One was that only a limited run at a premium price—higher than anyone had ever seen on a Sportsters—was done.

The other result was a bike that was a stunning performer. With 70 horsepower, this was a rocket through the quarter, crossing the line in 12.88 seconds. A booklet from the factory advised owners how to get another 30 horsepower from the engine. However, the price premium deterred sales. Only 1,018 sold in 1983, and just 759 sold in 1984 before Harley concluded that perhaps customers were not so anxious for a streetable XR-750.

In fact, customers *did* want a high-performance bike. They only preferred to have it without the high additional cost. An extra $2,000 that could be spent in aftermarket speed shops would produce the power of the most expensive XR-1000 and then some. Especially if the rider began the project with the least expensive Sportster ever, the XLX.

But for those 1,777 other riders, the logistics of tracking down the shops—and the inconvenience of being without the bike while the work was being completed—made the additional cost well worthwhile. Once again, it may have been the attraction of a fully factory-warranted rocket ship. Or maybe it was a matter of having the rocket ship *right now* versus waiting for it.

Above: Except for its slate grey finish, the XR-1000 closely resembled its racing cousin, the XR-750. Three large 11.5-inch disc brakes stopped the bike. Only 1,018 sold in 1983, and 759 sold in 1984 before Harley-Davidson ceased the bike's production.

Left: A "short track" 2.25-gallon tank offered another 0.25 gallon as reserve. This was adequate for quite a few quarter-mile dashes. Compression ratio was 9.0:1. The bike weighed 480 pounds without gas or oil. Wheelbase was 60 inches and seat height was just 29 inches. Ignition was of the electronic breakerless variety.

Chapter 16
Riding For the Brand

While hot rodders, auto enthusiasts, car wackos, and muscle car gearheads have "customized" their cars to fulfill their fantasies almost since Henry Ford rolled out his first Tin Lizzie, motorcyclists have not. There is an important difference in the terminology that refers to how these kinds of objects are made personal. There are particular words that define and explain what automobiles and motorcycles mean to their owners.

Motorcyclists certainly have changed handlebars, seats, tires, and paint. They've gone inside the engines and done major modifications up to and including rendering them very nearly unrideable. They have replaced the carburetors, exhausts, and wheels. They have lengthened their bikes, raked the, extended and lowered them. They have added—or deleted—fenders and lights, bags, and seats for two, and backrests for sissies. And they have chrome-plated everything from bolts to frames.

It has always been an individual's choice. This work done to further identify, describe, and —yes—to show off the personality of the owner. But it has not been "customizing." While car people customize, motorcyclists "personalize."

Probably one of the best artists working in the medium of the personal motorcycle is Arlen Ness, based in San Leandro, California, just south of Oakland on San Francisco Bay. Ness' influence has spread far beyond Oakland or even the West Coast. He creates, designs, invents, builds, manufactures, and then mail orders. His catalog is a wish book for enthusiasts with imagination. With his influence, personalized motorcycles exist across North America and throughout Europe. Ness' success and his ideas have spawned hundreds of comparable artists. Many of these perform aftermarket installations of Ness pieces; others create their own work, frequently of exceptional quality and imagination.

Above: An adjustable suspension and swingarm by Progressive allows nearly two inches of ride height flexibility. Harley-Davidson Softail Customs had hard engine mounts even though the FLT introduced the rubber-mounted engine in 1980. A five-speed transmission operated through the rubber belt final drive, and under-frame shock absorbers allowed riders to look "hard" while riding "soft."

Opposite: Custom paint is as important on personalized bikes as chrome. Precision Motors of Oxnard, California, emblazoned this custom Softail with its bright blue and red. The rendition of Crazy Horse monument was painted by Born Again Fairings of San Dimas, California. Total investment in this bike is around $23,000, including the motorcycle.

Opposite Page Top: It wasn't an uncommon bike to begin with, the Softail Custom. Harley-Davidson sold 6,621 of them in 1988. But for many years since World War II, it's not been just about what Harley did to its bikes but what its buyers did to their bikes. In this case, the basic Big Twin Eighty was turned over to White Bros. Accessories for a stroker kit, stretching the engine out to 89 cubic inches.

Opposite Page Bottom Left: Rev-Tech wheels hold 3.00x21.00-inch front tires and 5.10x16.00-inch rears beneath the custom-fabricated front and rear fenders. Disc brake rotors were chromed. The bike was given a fully belly pan and air dam behind the front wheel.

Opposite Page Bottom Right: About 85 horsepower come out of that chromed and polished twin. A Morris magneto, Screamin' Eagle carburetor and air cleaner, Jerry Branch heads, Crane cam, Barnett clutch, and Supertrapp exhaust rounded out the performance end of this personalized package.

Below: Arlen Ness fairings, handlebars, hand grips, and rearview mirrors, along with his foot pegs are blended with custom-molded tanks and frame, front and rear fenders, and a custom seat by Corbin. Factory Softails placed springs and shock absorbers along the bottom of the frame behind the engine. This retained the looks of the early hardtail frames but allowed a softer ride.

Leading a completely different direction is Erik Buell, a former engineer in both the racing shops and in production bike development at Harley-Davidson who left to build his own bike. Buell was involved in developing the rubber belt drive that appeared first on the Sturgis Eighty. He began producing his own machines using Harley-Davidson engines but he set them into a chassis meant more for canyon and café racing. His goal was something more like a modern-day XLCR. His current Thunderbolt looks more like it was designed in Milan, Italy, than in Milwaukee, U.S.A. However its engine—and its uncorked sound—are unmistakable, even if his bike is not yet accepted by Harley traditionalists. His machines are highly functional in a drastically different direction from the company's main line. Yet they are well enough regarded in Milwaukee that Harley-Davidson now owns half of Buell.

However, this is not about the success of personal bike makers. It has to do with the vision of any bike owner, the secret identity in every rider as they imagine themselves cruising or racing or parking and posing. The motorcycle—especially the "personalized" Harley-Davidson motorcycle—has gone far beyond the Davidsons' and Harley's initial idea of basic transportation.

There is an expression that is used among cowboys. It is said that a cowboy "rides for the brand." This is different from

Above: The FXRP was the police version of the fairing-equipped FXRT, similar to the earlier Low Rider with the addition of a frame-mounted fairing. Braided aircraft-type hoses feed the Dell'Orto two-barrel 40mm carburetor while Arlen Ness exhaust pipes snake around the stock but polished cases. Builder Bob Peiffer of Washington, Iowa, rebuilt it from a collection of parts in a crate.

Opposite: This customized 1990 FXRP was lowered, its front forks shortened by four inches. A custom front air dam was fabricated and fitted to deflect air up onto the massive cooling fins of the Evolution engine. This is the modern descendent of every 45-degree Harley-Davidson Big Twin that had come before. A Danny Gray seat sinks the rider deep into the frame.

Right: Otis Chandler's first vehicle, a used Harley-Davidson Knucklehead, was purchased in 1953 while he was in college.

Above: Delta Black, Tourglo Yellow, Too Cool Blue, and Hot Pink Pearl decorate this personal statement. The front Metzeler tire is 3.25x19 and the rear Dunlop is 5.10x16. Despite its fine looks, this was a bike meant to go as well as show. Tested on a dynamometer, it developed 82 horsepower and it produces its power over the entire engine range beginning with low-end off-the-line torque to top-end horsepower.

Opposite Top: Because customizers can do anything—there are no rules—mechanically, builder Peiffer left the Harley-Davidson pieces pretty much alone. He used cases, valves, lifters, ignition, transmission, sprockets, shifter, steering head rake, and front and rear brakes that are all standard Harley-Davidson Softail Custom. Then he picked these up and put them—as well as the factory-issued solid rear wheel—onto his bike.

Opposite Bottom: The Low Rider measured 66.3 inches of wheelbase. Seat height on this bike is just under 24 inches compared to 26 inches stock. Weight without fuel or oil is around 600 pounds. The Low Rider came from Milwaukee with a five-speed transmission and rubber belt final drive.

merely riding for a job, for a paycheck. It is a kind of loyalty beyond what can be bought. For these riders, there are no whole days off. For these riders, the basic questions of life boil down to two issues: Do the cows come first or does the earth? Some say it's the cows because they are what pay them the reward at the end of two years of raising them, fixing them, roping them, and branding them. Others say it's the earth because the earth supports the cows. But wherever that debate stops, they know that they are third. Cowboys who ride for the brand take the attitude that they own the place they work for and that every single cow counts. Cowboys who ride for the brand are rather like the Native Americans who preceded them. They understood why extreme loyalty can exist to something that is outside of themselves but that has so much influence over them.

What does all this have to do with Arlen Ness and Erik Buell and Harley-Davidson?

Everything.

More than any other product made by humans, Harley owners ride for the brand. No one tattoos Buick Electra or IBM/PC or Rolex or Sony Trinitron or Steinway Piano across their chest or back. Or across their stomach or down the inside of their thigh. Harley-Davidson is a brand like the one burned into a calf's flank. It has a loyalty unmatched by nearly any other product and envied by most. For Harley-Davidson riders, every Harley counts. Emotionally, spiritually, there are no whole days off.

Erik Buell's take on the Evolution 1200cc Sportster. Bore and stroke are Sportster stock 3.50x3.81 inches. Stock compression is 9.8:1. Stock output is 66.6 horsepower. But here, owner Bernie Stewart has deviated even from Buell's norm. An S&S Super G carburetor feeds fuel into Carl's Speed Shop heads. Solid lifters, Axtell pistons, and custom cams help Stewart see 78 horsepower from 13:1 compression.

Opposite Top: There is an unwritten mandate about Harley-Davidson. Basically, it says: "Be different. Do it your own way." Erik Buell applied that mandate and produced an excellent handling bike built around a stock Sportster engine. But owner Bernie Stewart took the mandate and turned things again, making the Buell into his own bike, one meant for the quarter-mile on Saturday nights. Stewart replaced the horizontal damper with a solid bar. In effect this made the Buell a "hardtail," making the power transfer more effective for drag racing.

Opposite Bottom: The essence of Harley-Davidson is its personal appeal. It's the invitation inherent in ownership to make it one's own. Former Harley engineer Erik Buell took that to heart and set out in the late 1980s to produce his first bike, the RR-1000, using an XR-1000 engine clothed in full bodywork. His RR-1200 followed in 1988 using the Evolution 1200 engine mounted beneath the RR-1000 body panels. The RS-1200 came next and used Buell's own frame with cutaway bodywork to reveal more of the engine. This third generation, the S-2 Thunderbolt, remains a road racer's Harley with plenty of power and fine balance for handling and cornering. Buell was successful enough that in 1994 Harley-Davidson made the Buell Motor Company a partially owned subsidiary of The Motor Company.

Top Right: Phoenix enthusiast Bernie Stewart traded his FLT dresser for the Buell Thunderbolt and then began to strip it and modify it for serious drag racing. He has shed the rear suspension, signals, and anything else that didn't help it go fast, cutting the bike's weight to 420 pounds.

Bottom Right: The factory Buell is belt-drive. Buell worked on that development during his years in Milwaukee. Stewart replaced it with a chain because belt windup at the drag strip made the bike into a lethal slingshot drive. In addition, he replaced the rear suspension, undermounted coil-over shock with a solid strut made of chromoly. For weight transfer, he lowered the front end 2.5 inches.

Chapter 17
Factory Mystique

F-head.
Flathead.
Knucklehead.
Panhead.
Shovelhead.

It was a litany representing the evolution of V-twin two-cylinder engines from Harley-Davidson.

And now for 1984 the Blockhead. The evolution has yielded The Evolution. The V2, a factory-stylized designation for the evergreen 45-degree V-twin. Its cylinders were aluminum alloy, no longer cast iron. It had a new head with new valves allowing a more direct intake and exhaust flow. It had electronic ignition. It was installed in a few magazine-test, pre-production models in late 1983 for the 1984 model year. It was tight, polite, reliable, and powerful. It would propel a 762-pound test bike to 96 miles per hour, far enough past the national fuel-economy speed limit to merit at least a weekend in jail. And in the magazine test, it provided a frugal 47 miles per gallon, efficient enough to merit early release for good behavior. If that wasn't enough, the engine was also mounted on three hard synthetic-rubber bushings. (This had been introduced in the 1980 FLT—touring models—and many riders think the mounts are rubber, sometimes resulting in the nickname "Rubber Glide.") This was done to isolate the vibrations of engine from the rider, diminishing the legendary shake that all those Harley-Davidson owners of yore had so cheerfully paid for over the years.

Within half a year of introduction, these new Blockhead engines also got wet clutches—diaphragm clutches—bathed in oil for cooling and providing plenty of splash for lubricating the primary drive chain. (Yes, the belt drive had succeeded as a final drive system. But engine heat destroyed the primary belts on

Above: Every motorcycle rider knows the truth of the motto on the tank cap. There is no myth here. If it is true that the mystique of Harley-Davidson is its heritage of 90 years in business, then the luxurious Heritage Softail with its polite comfortable road manners is one reason for the truth of the motto.

Opposite: The Heritage Softail was introduced in mid-1986 and was described in Harley-Davidson literature as a "recreation of a classic style of motorcycle." As historian David Wright has put it, "it brought back history with reliability." The stylistic debt to the Hydra-Glide bikes of nearly 40 years earlier is obvious.

some of the Sturgis models. The company reasoned a best-of-both-worlds policy was wisest, and the primary was replaced by chain while the best final drive was retained outside.)

As fine as the Blockhead was—so named by *Cycle World* magazine writers because of the polished metal shoe-box-top-like head—there was another innovation that was introduced that may have had even more impact on riders.

Harley-Davidson introduced a model with new letters at the end: ST, for Softail. Designed by an outside engineer, Harley saw the system where springs and shocks were placed horizontally beneath the gearbox and the entire rear end pivoted just under the rider's seat. Its aesthetic appeal was its appearance of the old hardtail bikes. If ever there was a company that worked hard to improve its past, it was surely Harley-Davidson. They didn't bother rewriting history. They simply looked it up, revised and improved it, and put it back on the market.

So in mid-1986, Willie G. Davidson's design department took another large leap away from the mainstream. The company introduced the FLST Heritage Softail, a 1950s throwback, delivered with a big, wide, comfortable seat.

Front spring-fork suspension was resurrected in 1988. Before telescopic tubes there was William Harley's college suspension project, an effort to soften the wrist-cracking ride of previous leading-link front fork design. Telescopic tubes were used, however, on the Fat Boy, a style statement introduced in 1990. Its Softail provided the hard look with a comfortable ride but the rest was a time-warp. Solid front and rear wheels gave a kind of l930s industrial look to the bike, dramatically aided by its staggered, over-under separate exhausts. It was 1930s streamline-era styling without radical sweeps and angles. And it was all silver with only

Above: The Evolution engine—nicknamed the Blockhead because Harley engines have always had nicknames inspired by the shape of the heads—contains 1,340 cubic centimeters. It has electronic ignition. The final drive is via a belt. It costs around $14,000. That is still less than the price of many new cars. Just like the prices in 1965—or even in 1903.

Left: Here is the myth and the mystique of Harley-Davidson. But it's anyone's guess which is which. The 1993 Heritage Softail is in the foreground, and the 1965 Electra-Glide is in the background. Willie G. Davidson has said that Harley's legacy is its mystique. Who would know better?

Left: The 80 ci V2 Evolution engine, introduced in 1984, made the Heritage Softails into the reliable, powerful time-travel machines that Harley-Davidson has marketed ever since. The Heritage weighs 710 pounds without fuel or oil on a wheelbase of 64.2 inches. Seat height is only 27.25 inches while overall length is 93.8 inches.

Opposite page: Introduced in late 1985 for the 1986 model year, the XL-883 Evolution Sportster carried on the original 883cc dimensions from the Sportster's 1957 introduction. Bore and stroke remained 3.00x3.81 inches, but output was now up to 53 horsepower. Shortly afterwards, the XLH-1100 was introduced. On the XLH-1100 bore was increased to 3.35 inches and horsepower went up by 10. The dual exhaust with a crossover that had been introduced on the Evolution Big Twins in 1984 was introduced on the Sportsters as well to equalize back pressure and to help the new Sportster pass the increasingly stringent noise requirements mandated by the Environmental Protection Agency.

Below: Dustin Hoffman, acting in a 1965 film, was assured by a guest at his own college graduation party that the future belonged to plastic. In that time, it did. But before the days when everything was improved with plastic, seats and saddlebags were made of leather. When Harley introduced the 90th Anniversary Heritage Softail, leather returned.

Racing Does Improve the Breed

Sometimes it is a great thing to have an opportunity to see into the future. It gives one the benefit not only of 20/20 hindsight but it also offers an unfair advantage against the competition.

Factory racing for Harley-Davidson has been a bittersweet experience during the past 80-odd years it has been in competition. The Wrecking Crew of the late nineteen-teens was much like getting extra maraschino cherries on top of the whipping whipped creame on the dessert. Harley's eight-valve engines dominated racing in the United States and then went to England and Europe and set records and reset European perspectives.

Opposite: In the pits before practice, Harley-Davidson 1994 team rider Miguel Duhamel, sitting on his VR-1000, talks with racing manager Steve Scheibe. The orange right side/black left side bodywork is carbon fiber and covers an aluminum twin-beam frame.

Below: Overall the VR-1000 is 79 inches long on a 55.5-inch wheelbase. Fuel capacity is 4.5 gallons, and the engine holds 3 quarts of oil. The final drive chain gets its power through the clutch from a new gear-driven primary drive system. The twin exhausts leave the left side of the barrels, cross under the frame ahead and join into one large canister-type muffler. This is the end of the bike Duhamel hoped most Superbike competitors would see.

Then there was a period when things didn't go so strongly in Harley's favor. After the eight-valves there was the D-series, brilliant at going up hills. Then there was the war. After that—but before the KRs of the late 1950s and the XR-750s of forever—there were the WRs. Racing has always been indulged in for two reasons: first it served as a high-pressure proving ground for new ideas and technologies; second it brought enthusiast attention to the company name (or more recently, the sponsors' names). When either of those goals is not met, racing stops.

So in 1994, Harley-Davidson enthusiasts got a chance to witness a third purpose for racing—to glimpse a technological future. As the world becomes smaller, as concerns such as air quality and the intrusion of loud noise into privacy and quiet become greater, more creative solutions must be devised. The concerns of large groups have a way of becoming law.

Harley-Davidson campaigned a new racing motorcycle in the AMA National Superbike series, a 10-race series that began at Daytona in March 1994. This bike, the VR1000, was a showpiece, if not in its winner's-circle finishes, certainly for its technology and creativity. Of course, the engine was a V-twin, of 996cc. But it was

Opposite Top: Somewhere inside is the 60-degree V-twin with bore and stroke of 3.86x2.60 inches for total displacement of 996cc. Compression ratio is 11.6:1. Fuel feed is by a Weber electronic fuel injection system. The heads have four valves per cylinder, operated by chain-driven dual overhead cams. The water-cooled engine is reportedly very smooth from 5,500 up to redline at 10,200 rpm.

Opposite Bottom: Duhamel waits on the wall, talking with a friend while team mechanics make final adjustments before a qualifying session at Sears Point International Raceway in Sonoma, California. Duhamel raced alongside factory-supported privateer Fritz Kling throughout the 10 1994 AMA National Superbike race series.

Below: Working under an orange glow inside the team tent, race mechanics finish between-sessions reassembly under the watchful eyes of racing manager Steve Scheibe (standing right rear). With this Superbike entry, Harley-Davidson returned to—and updated by 70 years—its legendary eight-valve racing technology.

Road racing has been described by its participants as a series
of drag races punctuated by turns. Here Duhamel streaks
along racing his shadow, bending the curves into slightly
longer straights. His riding style throughout the season took full
advantage of the fine road manners on a bike some described as
down on power.

a 60-degree version. It was fuel injected and water cooled. It was fitted with dual overhead camshafts and given four valves per cylinder. In the press information released with the bike, Harley-Davidson quoted 135 horsepower at 10,000 rpm. What is really produced is unpublished, a confidential racing secret.

Its transmission has five speeds, its final drive is by chain. Its frame is aluminum, a twin-beam perimeter-style with an adjustable swingarm pivot, the better to tailor it to individual tracks and conditions. Its front fork is the inverted type, allowing 4.7 inches of travel (rear is 5.3 inches, accommodated by a single shock). The bike, dry, weighs 390 pounds.

Its bodywork is made of carbon fiber. Its brakes are dual disks in front, a single in back, made by Wilwood, the same U.S. company providing stoppers for most CART-IndyCar racers. Fifty of the bikes were produced—three as team racers—to homologate it (that is, legally qualify it) for racing. The VR1000 is the result of five years of conception, invention, development, and testing. And of five years of commitment.

Racing has always improved the breed at Harley-Davidson. And it has sparked some memorable road-going motorcycles and some major technological improvements in the bikes that followed. What Willie G. and his stylists take and what the engineers may absorb from the VR1000 is anyone's guess. But knowing Harley-Davidson's past, watching the VR1000 may be a glimpse of the future.

Below: Capably assisted by Wilwood racing disc brakes, Duhamel stayed on the power later than his competitors. Wilwood dual front discs used six-piston calipers for immense stopping power, coupled to a smaller rear disc with a dual-piston caliper. Wilwood makes brakes for CART IndyCars capable of 240 miles per hour and weighing upwards of 1,100 pounds. For Duhamel's 390-pound, 160-mile-per-hour bike, the advantage is obvious.

a bit of yellow trim on the rocker covers. Only a few were built, creating an instant mystique from a company that had obviously begun to really understand the word.

To further prove that it understood the importance of its history, H-D introduced the 1993 Heritage Softail Nostalgia, complete with whitewall tires. It wore real leather saddlebags and saddle with hair-on cowhide trim (which was the origin of the nickname "Moo Glide" or "Cow Glide").

Harley-Davidson evolution touched the Sportsters as well. In 1986, another new model, the XLH-883 was introduced. Cylinders and heads were plain aluminum, not cast iron like the XLX nor some rare alloy of unobtanium from the XR-750. Inside the engine, it reflected the learning and experimentation and accomplishments and developments of the new Evolution V2 Big Twin engines. The engine was physically smaller, it weighed less, and it had 29 fewer moving parts than its cast-iron predecessors.

Less than two months later, the company introduced the XLH-1100. Both engines used hydraulic-lifters just as the V2 had. Both Evolution Sportsters were served up a time when the Japanese motorcycle market was strong. Harley-Davidson set a $3,995 price on the 883cc Sportster in any color so long as it was

It is still the affordable way to get a Harley-Davidson. Base price in 1994 for the basic Sportster was $4,873. But surveys showed that most owners quickly spent an additional 10 to 15 percent to personalize the bike to their taste. With a peanut tank and solo seat from the factory, it's easy to figure where the first dollars went.

black or red. This low price was set to induce riders to walk into the showroom while the 1100cc version, with 63 horsepower, sold for $5,199, $2,000 less than the nearest Big Twin, the no-frills FXR. A year later, the company lowered the bike, relocating and further tilting the rear shocks. This version was named the Hugger, implying it hugged the ground. It was also meant to embrace a new market segment made up of riders of generally smaller physical stature than traditional Harley buyers. It was meant to sell to women.

In 1988, the 1100cc engine was bored out, increasing its displacement to a full 1200cc. In its 494-pound factory fit, it would get itself—carrying half a tank of gas and a rider—to 60 miles per hour in four seconds flat. If the rider kept on going another block or so he would have covered a quarter-mile in 13 flat. Nothing standard from the automotive world that cost less than $100,000 would do that in 1988. Harley-Davidson had dropped that "C"

from the XLH designation. This was no longer a California-dealer designation. And it very certainly was still "hot."

By 1992, Sportsters had five-speed transmissions and belt drives, just like the Big Twins. The Hugger seat was lowered another one and a half inches to become a Super Hugger. The factory options list for the XLH-1200s became as large as those for the Big Twins.

Sportsters still have their engines rigidly mounted to the frames, and more than a few Sportster owners proclaim that they paid for all that vibration, and they want every bit of it. Harley-Davidson assures motorcycle journalists that there are no plans to stop the shake.

In fact, Harley-Davidson goes to lengths to reassure both journalists and riders that it has no plans to change anything. For a company to remain in business for nearly a century selling, at first, basic transportation and now something that is so much more means that Harley-Davidson has been doing it right. But doing it right is not always right for every rider or for every part of the world.

Willie G. Davidson, Vaughn Beals—Harley's Chairman who led the quiet, determined group to buy back Harley's freedom from AMF—and every other employee and manager and

The alloy cylinder barrels were fitted with iron liners but topped with alloy heads with a single intake and exhaust valve per head. The overhead valves were activated by hydraulic lifters. The forged one-piece-style flywheels of the second series XR-750 race bikes beginning 1972 were adopted for the new Evo engine. Except for pistons, valves and bore diameter, the 883 and 1200 engines are identical. This is the 883.

executive within the company have chosen carefully who they welcome to their stores. It's not discriminatory. It's American.

In America, racing among professionals has mostly been round left turns that are interrupted by flat-out, full-throttle sprints along a straightaway. During the past three decades, American racing has also accepted right turns and jumps. But racing in America has also been from one set of lights—stop-and-go or Christmas tree—to another set a quarter-mile away. When the U.S. Congress established the land-grant system in dozens of states west of Washington, D.C., to encourage population growth and national expansions, it set the stage for the kind of vehicles and passion and pleasures that American young men and women would pursue. The one-mile sections in Wisconsin and Colorado and Oregon gave way to President Dwight D. Eisenhower's interstate highway system. This was

ostensibly designed in order to assure speedy straight-line movement of military personnel and materiel from one coast to another if needed. It was approved in the mid-1950s. Within a few years, Cadillacs had fins the size of commercial airplane tails. A decade after the interstate was approved, Harley had the Electra-Glide.

When OPEC shut off the spigot on cheap gasoline to the United States and the rest of the world, Congress reacted by imposing a nationwide, strictly enforced 55 miles per hour speed limit. Neither cars nor motorcycles in America needed to go 140 miles per hour any longer. Nor did they need to be able to streak around mountain hairpin roads. Eisenhower had taken care of that too.

So Harley-Davidson has paid careful attention to who we are as residents of the United States. We long to reassume

control of our own lives and to re-acquire the independence of our youth. We hunger for involvement with our environment, and we thirst for experience. We are tied down to jobs and homes and families and to responsibilities that, in truth, most of us out there wouldn't change if we could.

So, for a few minutes a day, a few hours a week, a Harley-Davidson allows us to be Lee Marvin or Peter Fonda. Knowing that the motorcycle is in the garage or parked outside the window, knowing it is always there means that even if we cannot ride, we can think about it, fantasize a ride. It means that there are fewer really bad days. It is always there, offering ready escape.

On the motorcycle, chest and arms and head dragged by the wind, riders *can* be commuters. Or they can be the last American cowpokes, riding off into the sunset with a living thing breathing beneath them, taking no whole days off, riding for the brand.

Opposite: The Sportster Deluxe offers riders such as Bettina Chandler here a quick, smooth trip. The previously optional belt drive is now standard. For the 883, Mileage is reported to be better than 50 miles per gallon and top speed is around 112 miles per hour. In 1991, the company replaced the evergreen four-speed transmissions with five-speeds, bringing highway cruising speeds into a more comfortable engine-rpm range.

Above: Seat height is 30 inches, and its weight with full tanks is 478 pounds. The wheelbase is 60 inches. A neatly hand-lettered sign observed on a milling machine in the Milwaukee engine plant demonstrated where the Sportster fits in the hearts of Harley-Davidson employees. It read: "The Smallest Size We Build Is XL."

Epilogue
The Sweet Sound of the Open Road

"He stands very close to the bikes while the men start them, one by one setting up a deafening roar, a noise like a volcano buried under blacktop and beginning to erupt … and it seems to me they idle there longer than necessary, enjoying the disruption their machines make inside the early evening air … until one by one, Rango leading and Pete going last, they take off, a pack of cheetahs, bearing down on the curve of road that leads away from Jesse's house so fast I think they're going to skid, skid and crash and burn, but all they do is disappear, only their sound trails behind them."

West Coast writer Kristen McCloy wrote those words in her novel *Velocity*, a great steaming love story of a woman and a man and machines. It is a novel of heat and passion and mystique.

At idle, a Harley-Davidson is a cocky, arrogant thing. It stops conversation. It is rude, intrusive. It commands attention because it has interrupted everything going on around it.

Only one thing sounds better than a Harley-Davidson at idle. That is a Harley-Davidson going somewhere. Approaching. Passing. Disappearing. The sound that lives behind the rider's ears, the sound assaulting pedestrians on any street corner, the drivers inside any car. That sound. The sound of idle made urgent and purposeful and businesslike.

As many Harley riders will say, that is not noise. Other bikes make noise. Machines make noise. Big trucks and jet planes and buildings collapsing and trees falling in the woods when no one is there make noise. Harley-Davidsons make a sound like no other bike still in business. Other makers can manufacture bikes that look like Harleys, but no one has been willing to invite the vibration in order to produce the sound.

And it's that vibration that sets up the volcano beneath the blacktop, the roar of eight valves on high banking at Altoona, Pennsylvania, and B-17s over the North Sea. It's the vibration that brings up the front wheel on Main Street in Hollister and on the main straight at Daytona. It blasts the leaves at The Rock Store and tears at the smooth warm Sunday afternoon air in Malibu.

Imagine what would happen if hundreds of Harley-Davidsons rode over the San Andreas Fault all at once. Prudence would dictate an east-bound route, heading for that beach-front property in Reno and Phoenix. But Prudence doesn't ride a Harley.

Index